SHINING LIGHTS

Six Anglican saints of the
19th century

MARGARET CROPPER

DARTON, LONGMAN & TODD
LONDON

DARTON, LONGMAN & TODD LTD.,
64 CHISWICK HIGH ROAD,
LONDON, W.4

Printed at The Bowering Press, Plymouth

CONTENTS

MAIN SOURCES AND
ACKNOWLEDGEMENTS

Lord Shaftesbury. The three vol. Life by Hodder.
  Shaftesbury by J. L. and Barbara Hammond.

John Coleridge Patteson. The contemporary biography by his cousin Charlotte Yonge.

Christina Rossetti. Life by W. M. Rossetti preceding her Collected Poems.
  Christina Rossetti by Dorothy Stuart.

Edward King. Biography and Memoir, G. W. E. Russell.
  Spiritual letters, edit. B. W. Randolph.
  Edward King and Our Times, Lord Elton.

Mother Cecile. *Mother Cecile of Grahamstown*, by a Member of the Community of the Resurrection.
  Mother Florence, by a Member of the Community of the Resurrection.
  Short memoir by Margaret Robins.

Mary Brown. *Mrs John Brown*, edited by Angela James and Nina Hills.

I am grateful for the loan of the Biographies of Mother Cecile and Mother Florence from the English House of the Community of the Resurrection and, had it been possible to trace the owners of the copyright, proper acknowledgement would have been made to them. I should like to acknowledge the kindness of the Hon. Mrs James and John Murray Ltd in allowing me to make use of the only account of Mrs John Brown's life contained in *Mrs John Brown* edited by Angela James and Nina Hills.

FOREWORD

God's saints are shining lights
Henry Vaughan

The nineteenth century was a time of such enormous change and growth that it was hard to choose six saints who might express its particular sanctity. I have not succeeded in spacing my saints very well, and their lives have flowed over into the next century, but the sources of their inspiration belong to the nineteenth century.

One difficult thing in writing about these Victorian saints has been that there is often something that rather revolts us in their phraseology. We are not far enough away from it, and we are still conscious that some words and expressions have lost their force, for us without regaining a sort of authority which comes after a longer lapse of time.

It was a time of turmoil in religious thinking, but there are certain 'marks of the Lord Jesus' which shine out, holy, prophetic, with the 'Shining Light', which Bishop King required in those who worked for Christ. It was not difficult to find six saints but to choose six saints.

I chose Lord Shaftesbury because he is the saint of the Industrial Revolution, the man who because of his allegiance to Christ found intolerable what so many less inspired Christians were content to tolerate in the name of industrial necessity.

John Coleridge Patteson stands for the great band of heroic

ix

men who believed that the Gospel must be preached in all the world, and were prepared to suffer and die for that belief. The flame of his self-giving to the Melanesian Islanders shone out and lighted him to his martyrdom.

Mother Cecile of Grahamstown speaks for the Religious, feeling their way through the century to orders which should express the faith of the Anglican Communion, and carry forward the traditional life of the professed Religious. She stands in the forefront of these women in her astounding ability and courtesy, her endearing love of her sisters, and her grasp of the South African situation. The flame of her consuming love for Christ still shines on the altar where she worshipped.

I chose Christina Rossetti because the poems of a saint if they are also the poems of a real poet penetrate very deeply into the heart of the religion of the time. Many people found their way towards the expression of their devotion through her poems. She was their voice.

Edward King revolutionised in his own way the offices of deacon and priest in his training of men. He also brought a lovely humility, and intimate affection into his office as a bishop. The Oxford Movement came to a fine flower in his life.

Mary Brown stands for that call which came to women to serve in the causes which bettered the lives of the poor, lonely and lost. Into the temperance movement, into the Lock Ward, and the Workhouse, she brought the 'Warm wind' of the Gospel. To South Africa she gave her final experience of the Spirit.

But how many sides of the growth and essence of the Anglican Communion I have left out, how many of her saints, Keble, F. D. Maurice, Josephine Butler, the women who first followed Florence Nightingale.

One thing emerges in the study of the century. The turmoils, the controversies, the clashes in the life of a church and people do not prevent the saints from fulfilling their several vocations, though they may add to their sufferings, and sometimes bring about their martyrdoms. Those whose passion is to do God's Will, are enabled to do it, in spite of stormy seas, lions in the path, and the slime of greed and apathy.

LORD SHAFTESBURY

1801—1885

IT was the watch that brought it all back to him, to this rather careworn man with his interesting, quiet face. He took it out of his pocket to measure the time before his next engagement; his engagements were legion, and he often felt hemmed in by them. The watch had been part of his childhood, this slim gold watch which Maria Millis tucked into her comfortable bosom. She was stouter then than when she came from her home near Blenheim to be maid to the Countess of Shaftesbury, newly married, and she had graduated through the great household and was now housekeeper. She might look at the watch before calling little Anthony Ashley Cooper to bed, saying that she had just time to hear his prayer which she had taught him. She might look at it again when the prayer was said, and find there was still time for a story about Jesus. How close he always seemed to Maria as the little boy leant against her knee, and heard about someone, a Saviour, who really loved him, loved him as Maria loved him. These were the good moments in a childhood full of terror for the serious, sensitive child, whose mother was a fashionable, rather formidable, person and whose father believed in ruling his family by fear.

Maria knew what he would need in that unfriendly environment and she gave him Jesus, told him about the birth at Bethlehem and the 'dear hands that did such good', and the 'cross where he saved us all'. When she died, when Ashley was only eight years old and in the full misery of his first year at a cruel school, she left him her watch as a token of her love; and he had treasured it ever since. If anyone asked him about it, he said that it had been given to him by the best friend he ever had.

A respite had come, he remembered, when he was twelve years old and left the filth and cruelty and starvation of his first school for five happy years at Harrow. What he learnt at that first school was a sympathy for all children who were afraid or oppressed or hungry, a lesson that he never forgot. The unhappiness of unhappy childhood hit him hard. He knew about it from inside.

Well, as he thrust the watch back into his pocket and continued his crowded day, he blessed God for Maria, so simple, so loving, so faithful a lover of the Lord, who had given him a faith which was never to flinch in a long struggle against cruel conditions and indifferent people. And yet in a way it was a double-edged gift to him for he never could bear to think of the Christian faith as anything different from the faith which Maria had professed, and this made him sometimes very bitterly opposed to any other form of Christian worship. But Maria's gift was central in his life. 'She gave him', writes Canon Raven, 'a love of Christ which saved his loneliness from becoming egoism, his hardships from embittering him, which transformed his sensitiveness into compassion, his ambition into a desire to serve.'

He came of a distinguished family, this young Ashley—his father was the 7th Earl of Shaftesbury; none of the family had been negligible, and his mother was a Churchill from Blenheim; the blend of the two families might well produce something remarkable. Ashley was born in 1801 and his life nearly spans the century.

In the years at Harrow one incident stands out to which he later traced an impulse towards his vocation. The schoolboy Ashley, strolling along, heard drunken shouting and singing, and presently round the corner came four tipsy men carrying a dead pauper in his coffin. As they tried to turn, they lurched and the coffin fell, and they broke out into such profanity as the boy had never heard.

'Good heavens!' he murmured, 'Can this be permitted, simply because the man was poor and friendless?'

Maria to teach the love of God, the pauper funeral to teach the need of man! Before the drunken bearers and their dead man were out of sight, Ashley had determined that, with the help of God, he would from that time devote his life to pleading the cause of the poor and friendless. Years afterwards he was able to point out the exact spot to Dr Butler.

But an interval with a parson cousin in the country, where he gained very little, and three years at Oxford, where he achieved a first in Greats, lay between this moment and any fulfilment of his vow. His father's plan for him had been that he should take a commission, but finding that he had a son with brains he switched over to politics. And so Ashley entered his own special arena, where he was to fight so manfully his first battles as Conservative member for Woodstock, one of the Marlborough pocket boroughs.

He made a survey on his twenty-fifth birthday of his thoughts and hopes. He felt them to be neither wise, nor good, nor endowed with possibilities for becoming so. It was a lifelong habit this self-criticism, recorded in his diary, which he carried almost to a morbid extent, but which perhaps relieved his

3

anxious capacity to suffer. He remarks on the day-dreams since he left Oxford, 'Vision without end, but God be praised all of a noble character'. He had already pictured for himself a career valuable to his country. How valuable, but how different from his dreams and his young ambition it was to be! 'I will entreat God to raise up for old Britain young and aged saints and sinners, high and low, rich and poor, who may act as well for her interests as I always fancied I wished to do. . . . Latterly I have taken to hard study; it amuses me, and prevents mischief.' That there might have been mischief he knew well enough from a desperate love-affair he had had in Vienna, from which, however, he emerged unscathed.

Though he got into Parliament in 1826 as a Conservative, his first sessions were marked by a sort of independence which was to become characteristic. His hero at the time was the Duke of Wellington, 'Dukey' as he called him. It was loyalty to the Duke that kept him from taking a post in the Government offered to him by Canning, though he was at the time full of ambition and he cast a longing eye at the distinction.

> Time was (he wrote later), when I could not sleep for ambition. I thought of nothing but fame and immortality. I could not bear the idea of dying and being forgotten. But now I am much changed. . . . I desire to be useful in my generation, and to die in the knowledge of having advanced happiness by having advanced true religion.

But Canning did notice the promising young man, however independent he might be, and gave him a place as commissioner on the India Board. It was an astonishment to the other members that, when the question of suttee came up, Ashley should protest against the practice. 'I was put down as if I were a madman', he records in his diary. It was an experience that was often to be repeated.

About this time he made his first speech, in a low rather inaudible voice, but he chose one of the causes which was to hold him all his life long. Mr Robert Gordon was moving a bill asking for leave to amend the law for the regulation of lunatic asylums, and Ashley advanced into this rather terrible field in all his young gallantry. 'Last night I ventured to speak, and God be praised I did not utterly disgrace myself . . . and so by God's blessing my first effort has been for the advancement of human happiness.' But it led to his first taste of horror. When at last both Houses had passed an Act that had been struggled for since 1819, part of its set-up was a body of commissioners on whom a great burden of the work was cast. Ashley agreed to become one of the commissioners. It was a work that he was never to lay down, and it involved him in his first hand-to-hand struggle against inhuman behaviour. In 1834 he became chairman of the commissioners, a post that he kept till his death.

It was grim work that the young lord had undertaken. 'There is nothing poetical in this duty', he notes, and adds, 'Did not wish for such employment but duty made it imperative.' For the work involved visiting the asylums, and when, thirty years later, he gave an account of those early days every horrid detail was still clear in his mind: 'When we began our visitations, one of the first rooms that we went into contained nearly a hundred and fifty patients, in every form of madness, a large proportion of them chained to the wall . . . the noise and din were such that we positively could not hear each other. . . . I never beheld anything so horrible and so miserable.'

When they went on to the women's department it was worse: 'I do not think I ever witnessed brute beasts in such a condition.'

But the tall, grave, rather beautiful young man standing looking at these poor women had no idea of turning back on his course. He was going to stand by them till at the end of his life.

> Half a century all but one year (he wrote in 1877) has been devoted to this cause of the lunatics, and through the wonderful mercy and power of God, the state now, as compared with the state then, would baffle, if description were attempted, any voice or pen that were ever employed in spoken or written eloquence. *Non nobis domine*. . . . How few had any notion of the years of toil and care that, under God, I have bestowed on this melancholy and awful question.

Some family events come between this first tilt against the devil and the Ten Hours' struggle which was in a way the greatest effort of his life. There was a quarrel with his father which kept him away from his home for many years, but there was also his exceedingly happy marriage. This was all the more wonderful because he had chosen as his bride a girl, Lady Emily Cowper, who came from a family not at all noted for seriousness or religious stability. Creevy described her as 'the leading favourite of the town so far', her family thought it a very odd match, though they came to be very fond of Ashley and he was often at their home at Panshanger. His wife became absolutely one with him in his ideals and his religious life. In 1839 when they had been married for nine years, he wrote:

> It is a wonderful accomplishment, and a most bountiful answer to one's prayers, to have obtained a wife in the highest matters and the smallest details after my imagination and my heart. Often do I recollect the very words and sentiments of my entreaties to God that he would give me a wife for my comfort and improvement and safety. He has granted me to the full all that I desired, and far more than I deserved.

6

They must have been a distinguished-looking couple. An old friend, Lord Granville, wrote of Ashley at this time: 'He was a singularly good-looking man, with absolutely nothing of effeminate beauty. He had those manly good looks, and that striking presence, which I believe help a man more than we sometimes think; and they helped him when he endeavoured to inspire his humble fellow-countrymen with his noble and elevated nature. Those good looks he retained to the end of his life.'

Another description of him says:

He is above the medium height, with a slender and extremely graceful figure . . . his curling dark hair in its thick masses resembles that of a sculptured bust, and his fine brow and features are distinctly and delicately cut; the nose perhaps a trifle too prominent to be handsome. He has light blue eyes deeply set and near each other . . . his mouth is small, retiring and compressed.

His connection with the Cowper family came to have a special importance in his life, as his wife's mother married Palmerston as her second husband and the two men became real friends and allies.

As he comes up to the great fight over the Ten Hours' Bill, what is in his own mind? He had put down on his twenty-seventh birthday some considerations which were to guide him all through his life: 'Now let me consider awhile my future career. The first principle: God's honour, the second: man's happiness; the means: prayer and unremitting diligence. All petty love of excellence must be put aside, the matter must be studied, and one's best done for the remainder.'

Something of the misery of his childhood had left him with an inferiority complex which always haunted him. He did fall into the snare of analysing his own life too much. I think it was peculiarly an Evangelical snare, and he felt himself so lonely in his work. In these young years he turned to science and especially to astronomy, having made friends with the astronomer South. But this was just a feeler after a vocation, though the following passage shows how much he was moved by it:

> Last night I spent at South's in observation of the heavens. I was enraptured. I may be a wicked man, and one regarded by God as deceitful upon the weights, but still there is within me a spirit of love and adoration which bursts forth at the sight of Nature's glories. My soul is so filled that it cannot find vent but in aspirations towards a higher Being. . . . As for myself, my heart is so touched when I view the sweet magnificence of the Creator that I could fall to weeping in tears of gratitude and joy. Had two or three walks on the cliff (at Brighton); had an opportunity of what I love, a silent prayer in solitude and contemplation . . . I love the sea. I see the works of the Lord, and His wonders in the deep.

And this is the sensitive spirit that God chose to discover and bear and change an evil and heartless system; not once but over and over again. 'I will show him how great things he must suffer for My Name's Sake.'

When the Napoleonic war ended, there were almost as many terrible things happening in England as there are now, in a different category, but witnessing to the evil of War. As now, there was a new set of circumstances to be reckoned with and a lack of courage, a sense of fatalism. Yes, we know these things are hideous, but what can we do? And a strange new god had crept into the reckoning of men—the god of economic necessity. He demanded the sacrifice especially of small children.

Ashley in a speech once said: 'He had read of those who had sacrificed their children to Moloch, but they were a merciful people compared with Englishmen in the nineteenth century.'

It was a deep and fatal idolatry that seized the England of the first half of the nineteenth century. Set up against it there were a few leaders who recognized other loyalties; Ashley was one of them and his loyalty was the one that Maria Millis had taught him, the loyalty to Christ. As every night he said the prayer which Maria had taught him, the indignation and the compassion of Christ steadied him against all the devices of the devil of disappointment, delay, loneliness and morbid self-pity. Ashley, like Wilberforce, felt that the servant of God is not at liberty.

He came into the great assault on the bad conditions in the factories when the fight had been raging for some time. He read in *The Times* (*The Times* was often his signpost) some extracts from the evidence given to a committee set up at the instigation of Mr Sadler, the member for Newark. He had somehow missed the debate on the evidence in the House, but he learnt now of Joseph Hebergan, aged seven, who worked from five in the morning till eight at night with a solitary half-hour's break at noon; of three little sisters all under ten who, in busy seasons, worked from three a.m. to ten-thirty p.m.; of another little boy who was so deformed as the result of his work that he could hardly pull himself up the three steps to his father's door. 'I was a poor man', the father said, 'and could not afford to take him away'; of two hundred families visited in Bradford who all contained deformed children owing to a certain action necessary to the weaving, so it was said. Ashley, full of disgust and horror as he read this sort of evidence, wrote to Sadler to ask if he could help him in any way. But he had no answer; Sadler's seat at Newark had been abolished by the Reform Bill and he had lost the seat in Leeds which he had contested. The stalwarts of the movement, Oastler, Bull and Wood were searching desperately for someone to be responsible for seeing the precious Ten Hours'

9

Bill through Parliament. It was a Scottish member, Sir Andrew Agnew, who suggested Ashley and brought Bull to see him. 'I can perfectly recollect', wrote Ashley some years later, 'my astonishment and doubt and terror at the proposition.' A quick decision was necessary. He consulted a friend or two, and then 'I went home . . . to decide for myself after meditation and prayer, and divination as it were by the word of God.'

It was a momentous decision. 'On the one hand', writes Hodder, his earliest biographer, 'lay ease, influence, promotion and troops of friends; on the other, an unpopular cause, unceasing labour amidst every kind of opposition, perpetual worry and anxiety; estrangement of friends, annihilation of leisure, and a life among the poor.' He put the question to his young wife, who encouraged him to accept the burden, and so the next day he told Bull that he would be responsible for seeing the Bill through the House. Bull, in a circular letter to the Short Time committees wrote: 'As to Lord Ashley he is noble and benevolent and resolute in mind as he is manly in person. Ashley wrote to Oastler:

> I wish, I ardently wish, that some other had been found to undertake the cause; nothing but the apprehension of its being lost induced me to acquiesce in Mr Bull's request. I entertain such strong opinions on the matter that I did not dare as a Christian, to let my diffidence or love of ease, prevail over the demands of morality and religion.

He certainly took Blake's advice and 'did his work in fear and trembling'.

The Bill was passed only after seventeen years of ding-dong struggle. Bull's optimistic report of the reception given to Ashley's notice of motion was soon out of date. Other Bills were introduced as red herrings across the path. When the Commons were in a better mood, the Lords were obdurate, indeed the opposition in the upper House to all measures of factory and mines reform was consistently bad and frustrating to the reformers, and Ashley himself, when he found himself there as the Earl of Shaftesbury, discovered a most chilling sense of apathy and selfish opposition. He had a much lonelier period to face than Wilberforce. There was no Clapham sect behind him, and the leaders of the movement were prepared to take steps which he disliked and feared. Oastler, Fielden and Bull, though staunch reformers, did not speak his language or accept his standards. As for the workers themselves he wrote in a depressed moment, 'They forget all my labour of love in the middle course I took for their welfare. I won for them almost everything, but for the loss of that very little they regard me as an enemy.' But he held on, though this sort of thing occurs often in his Diary:

H writes me that the Factory Bill is suspended indefinitely . . . Suspended forsooth! and thus another year is added to the period over which wrong and violence are to reign without control! The whole of last session and the best of this utterly lost (1841): all the evidence will be stale, facts without point and cases out of date . . . Nevertheless, 'against hope I must believe in hope'; as I began in faith so must I continue, regarding difficulties as so many trials, and delays as essential to maturity.

When the Whig government fell, and the Conservative under Peel came in, Ashley's name was mentioned in regard to office. But he himself had made up his mind. The Ten Hours' Bill came first. 'I am bound by every obligation, human and Divine, not to allow myself to be placed in any situation where I may not be equally if not better, circumstanced to advance these great interests.' He never did take office though he had many chances of doing so. When he wrote to Peel he said: 'I have experienced a degree of pain I know not that I ever felt before in venturing to express a decided negative—it takes from me all the pleasure and much of the hope I have in public life; but there was no choice . . .' It was all the more noble a decision because Ashley was at this time very short of money. He had quite a large family, and a very small income. He wrote to the secretary of the Yorkshire Short Time Committee: 'I declined the acceptance of any place under circumstances that would impede, or even limit my full and free action in the advancement of that measure which I consider to be vital both to the welfare of the working classes and the real interest of the country.'

There were two more sets of child workers whom Ashley was trying to benefit during this period of his Parliamentary life; the children working in the mines, and the climbing boys who swept the chimneys of England. Children in the mines! How came they there? What a hideous thought! But there they were, doing three jobs for which their size and intelligence fitted them. They sat alone in the dark for hours, pulling the string that opened the little doors that ventilated the mines; they were harnessed to little carts which they pulled along full of coal, often on their hands and knees (the women did this work too) or they pumped water out of the mine, standing sometimes in water above the ankles for their stint of twelve hours. Perhaps the worst used were the little apprentices supplied by the work-houses and who had no one to defend them. Sometimes a miner would protest that his own child should not do the worst jobs. But no one protested for the little apprentices. In 1842 he suc-ceeded in getting a Bill passed ensuring that all women, children and apprentices were taken out of the mines. Ashley made a remarkable speech in the Commons—some members were moved to tears; Cobden who had always been rather suspicious of Ashley, crossed the floor of the House to wring his hand and said, 'I don't think I have ever been put into such a frame of mind in the whole course of my life as I have been by your speech'. The opposition to the Bill came in the Lords, and Lord Londonderry especially tried to spike Ashley's guns; but the Bill, though injured in the Lords, was passed in 1842, and was one of Ashley's blessed triumphs in defence of women and children.

The effort to stop the work of the little chimney sweepers took years to effect. The most respectable householders cheated flagrantly over it, magistrates would not take action, because their own chimneys were often swept in the same manner, and not until Ashley was an old man and Charles Kingsley's *Water-babies* had stirred people's imagination, was the ugly thing finally stamped out.

I suppose that when most of us think of Lord Shaftesbury, we think of his work for the Ragged Schools. One day in 1843, he was reading *The Times* and there found a letter about the Field Lane Ragged School. He had for a long time been miserable about the state of children in the slums of London. He had penetrated into terrible places, avoided by the police, in his anxiety to see how the little street urchins were lodged. It had produced in him a raging despair. Was there anything to do? How and where could he start? Now he read of some people who had started, who had collected seventy adults and children, and were encouraged by the increased numbers of scholars and their altered conduct, and who asked for help in two ways, financial and educational.

'I never read an advertisement with keener pleasure', he wrote, and he got into touch immediately with the promoters of the work, and in time went down to the school itself to see what was going on. Field Lane was in the heart of what was called

Jack Ketch's Warren, a very unsavoury place and dangerous too. But there he found the work going on that he longed after; people really getting at these utterly degraded and miserable crowds. He went often and used to sit by the teachers watching the motley assembly of scholars, sometimes speaking to them, often making a child happy by his loving concern and kind voice. The Field Lane School was in a rather poor way when he began to work for it, but after ten years he had reshaped its destiny. It had a free day school for infants, an evening school for youths and adults engaged in daily occupation, a women's evening school, industrial classes to teach youth's tailoring and shoe-making, and many other departments. He didn't originate either the Ragged Schools or the Ragged Schools Union, but he did give all that he had of influence and interest to their work; he had a deep respect for the teachers and workers, and a very warm love especially for the children. It began to dawn on him that these children, after a certain amount of elementary training, would have much more chance of leading valuable lives if they could emigrate. Soon he was speaking in the House about his little ragamuffins, and asking for a grant to help his emigration scheme. He received a rather meagre one, but supplemented it by gifts from his friends. The scheme was a great success; Lord Ashley's boys were sought after by employers in South Australia, and made good in many trades.

One of his most daring experiments was a sort of thieves' party. He had often wanted to meet these people face to face, and the City Mission arranged this curious evening.

He was invited by the thieves themselves, forty of the most notorious robbers and burglars in London signed a letter asking him to come. He was astonished, however, when he arrived, to find about four hundred men: 'From the swell mob', says Hodder, 'in black coats, and white neckcloths, to the most fierce-looking, rough, half-dressed savages he had ever seen.' They welcomed him, and they listened to the prayers which he and the Missioner Jackson, who was known as the thieves' missioner, made.

I was anxious to know what was the character of these thieves, (he wrote) some of them pickpockets, some shop-lifters, others of the swell mob—and exceedingly well-dressed some of them were— many of them however, had no stockings and some of them had no shirts. I wanted to know the great departments of roguery; so the Missionary said 'His Lordship wants to know the particular character of the men here. You who live by burglary and the more serious crimes will go to the right, and the others will go to the left'. About two hundred of the men at once rose and went to the right, as confessed burglars and living by the greatest crimes.

Well, he talked to them, and they to him, telling him just how it was with them. 'A number of the men gave addresses and any- thing more curious, more graphic, more picturesque, more touching, I never heard in my life; they told the whole truth, without the least difficulty and knowing they were there to reveal their condition they disguised nothing.' 'Will you ever come back to see us again?' they asked at the end of the meeting. And Ashley said 'Yes, at any time and at any place, whenever you shall send for me.' Perhaps it was just the feeling that he cared so much that produced the rather astounding results. Within three months, thirteen of them were starting a fresh life in jobs in Canada, and not much later, three hundred out of the party had either emigrated or were settled in new work and had given up their old trade. Possibly no one had ever cared so much for them before.

He had a special affection for his little ragamuffin boys. One of them stole the precious watch, but soon afterwards a sack was deposited at the door of his house containing a little boy, and the watch. Such faith had they in him, that he would do his best for the child and forgive the theft, and they were right. Some people feel it regrettable that he passed so much of the end of his life immersed in the Ragged School movement, but the picture of him among these children and the poor people depicting his unfailing care for them, has somehow sweetened the records of Christian charity.

One night he went down to the Ragged School at the George Yard:

A magic lantern had been purchased to interest the poor things, and I went down to have a talk with them, as a series of slides representing the Crucifixion of our Lord was to be exhibited. There were about four hundred people in the room, and the police told me that between four and five hundred were turned away. The interest in the pictures was intense, and I shall never forget their earnest excited faces, as the scenes in the sacred drama passed before them. The last picture represented our Lord standing beside a closed door, and the text at the foot of the picture was: 'Behold I stand at the door and knock'. The effect was startling— it seemed to bring the story home to every heart, and when I said, 'What you see here is going on at the door of every house in Whitechapel,' they were moved to tears. It was a revelations to them, and when I told them that if they would open the door He would come and sup with them, there was something so cosy and comfortable to them in the idea of it that they came pouring round me and thanking me.

There was a break in Ashley's life when his father died in 1851 and he succeeded to the title of Earl of Shaftesbury, and to much else which was a burden to him. 'Now', he wrote, 'I bear a new name which I did not covet; and enter on a new career, which may God guide and sanctify. If I can by His grace make the new as favourably known as the old name, and attain under it but to the fringes of His honour and the welfare of mankind, I shall indeed have much to be thankful for.'

In a summary that he made in his diary about this time he wrote rather despairingly:

> All use me, and all grow tired of me; but few can know the troubles I have endured—the sorrow of mind, the weariness of body; the labour I have undergone by day and night; the public and private conflicts; the prayers I have offered, the tears I have shed. Here, however is my consolation, that amidst frailities, and sins, trespasses and shortcomings, I have had one single object perpetually before me. It was God's grace that gave me the thought; God's grace that has sustained me hitherto, to have, in truth, but one end, the advancement of His ever-blessed Name, and the temporal and eternal welfare of all mankind. So closes my review. *Sursum corda*!

But he was not to leave the House of Commons without recognition of what he had done there. It was Sir Robert Inglis, Henry Thornton's friend, who said:

> I believe I speak the sentiments of the House generally when I say that Lord Ashley should not be withdrawn from the first ranks of this assembly, the scene of his labours and triumphs, without some parting expression of respect and regret. During the last fifteen years of Lord Ashley's Parliamentary life, he has been emphatically the friend of the friendless. Every form of human suffering he has, in his place in this House and especially every suffering connected with labour, sought to lighten, and in every way to ameliorate the moral, social and religious condition of our fellow subjects.

He went to the Lords rather miserably asking in his diary: 'Shall I ever be able to do anything?' But the next day he was moving the second reading of the Inspectation and Registration of Lodging Houses Bill, of which Dickens said that it was the best law that ever was passed by any English Parliament. The law was passed in the very same session, and later, when he moved the second Lodging House Bill he wrote: 'Wonderfully well received . . . my surprise knew no bounds, I had warmed "Nova Zembla". God has now placed me here, and I must and do pray that as my day so may my strength be.'

But there were other more startling and humiliating things that he had to face when he succeeded his father, and it is part of the man's sanctity that he didn't try to cover them. He began to look into the state of the housing in his inheritance and found it shocking. His diary records:

> Inspected a few cottages, filthy, close, indecent, unwholesome. But what can I do? I am half pauperised; and the debts are endless; no money is payable for a whole year . . . Every sixpence I spend —and spend I must on many things—is borrowed. Shocking state of the cottages; stuffed like figs in a drum. Were not the people as cleanly as they can be we should have had an epidemic; must build others, cost what it may. Surely I am the most perplexed of men . . . I have passed my life rating others for allowing rotten houses and immoral unhealthy dwellings; and now I come into an estate rife with abominations . . . and I have not a farthing to set them right.

But there were some things he could do. He put an end to the truck system of payment, and he did begin to build, helped by his sister. He did some nice friendly things too; giving prizes for garden allotments, having the rent dinner at his own house instead of at the inn, arranging evening classes for the young men, and a cricket club with part of his park as their ground; and he built a school for the children who couldn't get to school, and sent a Scripture Reader to work in the villages. It was tempting for his enemies to retaliate here, and they did so with a good deal of venom. But in his father's time he could do

18

nothing, and he had a struggle with debt to the end of his life.

He was conscious now that he had a following, and a reputation for effective action. Of course he did more than any man should have attempted; but what moving activity it was, often a night out with his Ragged School comrades rescuing boys from their wretched beds underneath the arches, going to common lodging houses to find young people he knew who had come down to bedrock. Anyone could get access to him at his house in Grosvenor Square. He used to set out with a carriage full of toys for the slum children he knew, and if he made a promise to a child it was always kept. Never feeling really easy in the House of Lords, he tended out of the many choices offered to him, to give his time to the personal work, to seek the society of the Ragged School teachers and leaders, and the Coster's club in Golden Square of which he became a member, buying himself a barrow and a donkey, and loaning it out to members going through hard times. It was tempting to pour out his love where it was received by answering love so unquestioning and sincere. A word perhaps ought to be said about the May meetings at Exeter Hall where he took the chair for so many good causes, the Bible Society, the Y.M.C.A., and many enterprises in foreign missions. But he didn't altogether desert his special vocation to secure good conditions for child workers. He spoke for the children in the brickworks, the children working in gangs on the land, and drove through reforms of their work.

The most difficult part of his life-work to assess, because it seems most alien to our thinking now, was his rampant Protestantism. When he was giving information to his biographer he wrote:

My religious views are not popular, but they are the views that have sustained and comforted me all my life. They have never been disguised, nor have I ever sought to disguise them. I think a man's religion, if it is worth anything, should enter into every sphere of life and rule his conduct in every relation. I have always been, and please God always shall be an Evangelical of the Evangelicals, and no biography can represent me that does not fully and emphatically represent my religious views.

He wanted to reform the Church as much as the Tractarians did; what he wanted was a practical, courageous Church, concerned with people's lives. Probably much of his thinking was governed by the fact that he had found the clergy as a body not interested in his work for shorter hours and better conditions. There were some whom he knew who did care, namely, Edward Bickersteth, George Bull, Canon Reeve of the Portman Chapel, but he felt that the majority of the clergy were losing their chances of getting into close touch with the working man. He wanted more power for the laity and less for the bishops and clergy. That was the basis of his attack on Convocation. As to the Tractarians they were, he felt, opening the door to Rome, and the Reformation was going to be set aside, and the Pope's aggressive division of England into Dioceses with bishops and archbishops must be resisted by meetings and speeches of the most violent character. One has to remember how corrupt the government of the Papal states had become, and how the Pope stood for all that Shaftesbury hated in oppression and poverty. But at the end of his life he made peace with his cousin Edward Pusey, and wrote most sympathetically to Manning when the Archbishop of Paris was assassinated. It seemed that Christ had complete control of his compassionate heart, and his devoted will, but not always of his mind. He was full of a prophetic instinct where there was oppression, cruelty, and unkindness; but it deserted him sometimes when considering religious opinions which he did not hold. A rather surprising thing was his hatred of the Salvation Army, which might have been after his own heart. For Moody and Sankey and their work he had a great admiration. Always his aim was to reach the people outside the pale of Church influence. Very dear to him was the law which at last permitted services in buildings other than churches. He was like all our saints in the nineteenth century, a tremendous reader of the Bible; it must not be touched, the Revised Version was a terrible blunder, and Biblical Criticism, of course, simply sacrilege.

What he did believe, with the whole force of his compassionate heart, was that 'Christ Jesus came into the world to save sinners', and what he delighted to see was a room full of derelict people finding that saving grace, and embracing the chances given to them of being remade. 'Christianity is practical', he used to say, 'it does things for people', and when his little rapscallions from the slums made good on the Training Ships that he procured for them, or as emigrants; when thieves and robbers took to honest trades, when the costers ceased to cheat, and took care of their donkeys, there was something holy afoot. 'Ragged Schools prizes last night', he wrote in his dairy, 'Talk of the Real Presence? Our Lord was as much there last night as at any time or place.' 'What the poor want', he used to say, 'is not patronage but sympathy.'

He did as a matter of fact, have a good deal to do with the church history of the mid-nineteenth century, for Palmerston as Prime Minister practically left the appointment of his Bishops to Shaftesbury, and between them, for a period they appointed those who on the whole were not sympathetic to the Trac-

C

tarians. Shaftesbury wanted bishops who would be friendly to the Nonconformists, and he wisely also wanted bishops who had been parish priests. Tait was perhaps the most notable of their appointments. 'There is no doubt of Tait's greatness as an Archbishop', writes Dr Moorman.

Something ought to be said about Shaftesbury's love for his family, and their very perfect relation to him. This man, whose own father and mother had been so cold to him, poured out his love on his own children, and had confident and easy relations with them. When his second son Francis was dying at Harrow, they were able to talk together about their faith quite simply and naturally. When he was choosing schools for his boys he wrote in his diary:

> I fear Eton; I dread the proximity of Windsor, with all its means and allurements; dread the tone and atmosphere of the school; it makes admirable gentlemen and finished scholars—fits a man beyond all competition, for the drawing-room, the club, St James St, and all the mysteries of social elegance; but it does not make the man required for the coming generation. We must have nobler, deeper, and sterner stuff; less of refinement and more of truth; more of the inward, not so much of the outward gentleman; a rigid sense of duty, not a delicate sense of honour; a just estimate of rank and property, not as matters of personal enjoyment and display, but as gifts from God bringing with them serious responsibilities, and involving a fearful account; a contempt for ridicule, not a dread of it; a desire and courage to live for the service of God and the best interests of mankind.

He lost three children before his wife's death, and his specially dear daughter, Conti, directly after. All these sorrows only brought him to a deeper faith.

His relations with his wife were very perfect. In 1872, not long before she died he wrote in his diary: 'Today my wedding day! Forty-one years ago was I united to that dear beautiful true and affectionate darling, my blessed Minny. What a faithful, devoted, simple-hearted and captivating wife she has been and is to me!' After she died he wrote one of her friends: 'She was my earthly mainstay, and cheered almost every moment of my existence by the wonderful combination of truth, simplicity, joyousness of heart, and purity of spirit. She was a sincere, sunny, and gentle follower of Our Lord.'

Quite soon after his wife's death, his eldest daughter died, and though her death was most beautiful and inspiring, it cost him much. But he crept back to work, first of all to his Coster friends at Golden Lane, writing to Mr Oarsman: 'I am very anxious to hear something about my people in Golden Lane. Give them my love and blessing and say that I shall, God willing, come to see them very soon in a quiet way. Thank them and the children for all their prayers.' He then set on foot as a memorial to his wife, a loan fund called after her, from which his watercress and flower-girl friends could borrow little sums to help them in the winter to get some little stock-in-trade. It was an imaginative plan, and the loans were nearly always repaid.

It was a year when the Public Worship Regulation Bill was being brought forward by Archbishop Tait. Shaftesbury, although he approved of its object, thought it gave too much power to the bishops. He was never very happy about bishops, though he helped Palmerston to appoint so many. He was much more in his element organizing a great meeting to protest against the use of Sacramental Confession, at one of the meetings which he swayed tremendously, ending his speech with words dear to himself and his wife 'Perish all things, so that Christ be magnified!'

But he had a kind word when Bishop Wilberforce, whom he

had so often opposed, was killed by a fall from his horse. 'Every kind feeling I ever had towards the Bishop is again alive. He was neither covetous nor hard, and he oftentimes stood forward in defence of the oppressed.'

Into these last ten years came his war against vivisection, his opposition to Disraeli's new title for the Queen as Empress, a deep concern about Bulgarian atrocities. Perhaps the most satisfactory thing to him, setting a seal on his long years of work in factory reform, was the Factory Consolidation Bill. Sir Richard Cross had skilfully combined all the factory legislation in one Bill. It was the completion of all Shaftesbury's labours. This was recognized when the Bill was passed in the Lords, and he writes in his diary: 'Nothing could exceed Beauchamp's kind and laudatory language of the measure, and of myself in the long course of forty-five years. He said everything that could please both principle and vanity.'

The diary is full of comments on his unpopularity and his many enemies, and it must have been a happy surprise to him when his eightieth birthday came, to find that it was celebrated almost as a national event. The idea sprang from the Ragged School Union, who wanted to honour him as their president, but it was widely taken up and there was a great meeting in the Guildhall. Inside the crowded hall were the grandees, M.P.'s, clergy, officials; but outside there was a still more moving assembly of flower girls, Ragged School children, costers, (with their donkeys and barrows) and the children crowded round him scattering flowers as he walked in. One thing that pleased him very much was a speech by W. E. Forster, not specially because he was a member of the government, but because he had been a mill owner in Yorkshire, who had known the evils of the factory conditions, and had been one of the first people to speak kindly

to him when he came to Bradford. In his speech Forster said:
'The good conduct on the part of the population was in a great
measure due to the moderating influences which were brought
to bear on them by Lord Ashley.' 'If anything is told of my life
after I am gone', said Lord Shaftesbury, 'let those words of
Forster's be recorded—I don't think in the whole course of my
life, any words every gratified me more.' As well as the public
ceremony there were a great many loving letters from every
sort of friend, from archbishops, and a cardinal, to the Ragged
School teachers and scholars.

Other happy afternoons in his last ten years were spent in
Dean's Yard where Dean Stanley allowed him to have the
annual flower show, for plants and flowers grown by the Ragged
School children and their parents, and his Coster friends in the
most unlikely places. It was on occasions like this that he himself gave great delight by talking to everyone, walking around
with the children holding his hands, and finding friends every-
where.

There was a revival of the work of suppressing the trade in
opium in these years, and in 1880 he became president of a
society concerned in it. Forty years before, he had made his
first attack on the evil thing, and he felt none the less violently
about it in his old age. 'I think there is not a single man who
believes one word of Revelation who will not agree with all of
us in saying that in its religious aspect it is altogether and un-
equivocally abominable.'

Anti-vivisection was one of his old-age causes. He sprang to
attention even in the 'eighties where there was a cry of cruelty
or exploitation. Then, just in the summer before he died he
became aware of the White Slave traffic: 'When the latest
phase of the subject was revealed', writes Hodder, 'he was

almost heartbroken that he had not the strength to stand forth as the champion of these poor children.'

'When I feel old age creeping on me, and know I must soon die', he said to a friend, 'I hope it is not wrong to say it, but I cannot bear to leave the world with all the misery in it.'

In the end he died in great peace down at Folkestone where he had gone to get the good sea air. His daughters were with him, and a devoted manservant, and there was a lot of quiet Bible reading, and a daily repetition of the Twenty-third Psalm. He asked to be buried at the little church at St Giles, his home in the country where his wife and daughter lay in the churchyard. But there was a service first in the Abbey, and all the way from his house in Grosvenor Square stood groups of mourning people, the poor and the destitute from all quarters of London. Outside the Abbey were deputations from all the homes and ships, schools, missions and charities all with their crêpe-draped banners.

As the funeral procession moved away from the Abbey 'a poor labouring man', writes Hodder, 'with tattered garments, but with a piece of crêpe tied on his sleeve, turned to one who stood beside him, and with a choking voice said: 'Our Earl's gone! God Almighty knows he loved us, and we loved him. We shan't see his likes again.'

Thinking of that life with so many fights, so many wounds, as his diary testifies, the mind goes back to the words in the Baptism service: 'I do sign thee with the sign of the Cross in token that thou shalt not be ashamed to confess the faith of Christ crucified, and manfully to fight under His banner against sin the world and the devil.' In his biography by the Hammonds, they write:

The devil with sad and sober sense on his grey face tells the rulers of the world that the misery which disfigures the life of great societies is beyond the reach of human remedy. A voice is raised from time to time in answer: a challenge in the name of the mercy of God, or the justice of nature, or the dignity of man. Shaftesbury was such a voice. To the law of indifference and drift taught by philosophers and accepted by politicians, he opposed the simple revelation of his Christian conscience ... When silence falls on such a voice, some everlasting echo still haunts the world, to break its sleep of habit or despair.

JOHN COLERIDGE PATTESON

1827—1871

THEY said in the little village of Alfington in Somerset that Bishop Selwyn of New Zealand was coming to preach. It was a great honour for their little church to have a bishop coming, but of course he was friends with the quality, and especially with the family of their Mr Patteson, who lived nearby, the young deacon who was curate at Alfington, and would be vicar when he got priested at Michaelmas. 'Oh, he was a proper gentleman was our Mr Patteson, so nice with the children, so comforting to the old and ailing, and kept the boys in order too; and to hear him in Church, well, his voice was as sweet as a russet apple. To do Mr Patteson credit all the children must be put into clean frocks and shirts for the Bishop's coming.'

They had all turned out for the evening service, that being the popular one, but those Alfington people would have been surprised if they could have known the tumult of thought that was going on in the mind of their Mr Patteson as he took the service. There he was, reading the service, in his beautiful moving voice as on so many other Sundays; but his whole life had been revolutionized since the previous Sunday, and he could scarcely attend to the Bishop's sermon, though reverently trying to do so. For he had disclosed that morning, in the hour after breakfast at his father's house, he smothered but overpowering wish to go to work with Selwyn in the Antipodes. Selwyn had begun it by asking him point-blank whether he was really happy working in that little parish? He had answered, a little vaguely, that later he might go to work in some big town, but that really —how strange the words sounded even to himself—what he wanted was to go out as a missionary, but his father, a widower, was delicate now and so dear to him, as were all his family, that perhaps he ought to set it aside while Judge Patteson lived. But Selwyn didn't see that; if he were really meaning to go, he should go while he was young and vigorous. Was he prepared to go anywhere? 'Yes, anywhere', he had replied.

It was really no new thing that had come to a head that day. It had been in his mind ever since the day when, seven years before as a boy at Eton, he had gone to Windsor Parish Church to hear Selwyn preach on the last Sunday before sailing for New Zealand. He had been tremendously moved that Sunday, so moved that he had spoken to his mother about it. Was it a call? And she had said that if it turned out to be a true call she would never hold him back. Yet she had been startled when Selwyn came to say goodbye to the Patteson family, old friends of his wife, and had said, prophetically as it seemed now: 'Lady Patteson, will you give me Coley?' (Coley; that was what they called him in the family. His mother was part of the great Coleridge clan that included the poet, and perhaps because it was his father's name, he had never been called John.) Through that rather disturbed Sunday there were family repercussions with his sister and step-sister and, more unnerving, with his father. It was only a few words exchanged, and the old man had said with his judicial clearness: 'It is my first impulse to say no, but that would be very selfish.'

'And now, to God the Father, the Son, and the Holy Ghost

. . .' The Bishop's voice rang out. That was the crux, of course
. . . not whether one wanted to go, but whether one was sent by
the Trinity of Love. Coley walked up to supper at his father's
house, and discovered that the Bishop had been talking to his
father, and after Sunday evening prayers he himself had another
talk with Selwyn. Then he got it straight from the shoulder, 'I
can no longer hesitate to invite you most distinctly to the work.'
They may have talked on, and Selwyn may have told the young
man what the situation was in the South Pacific. Selwyn himself
had not been many years in his diocese—which was as large as
England—before he discovered another and more baffling
responsibility which had, however, a romantic flavour about it.
There, on the fringe of his diocese of New Zealand was a chain
of enchanting islands, coral reefs with their dazzling whiteness,
blue harbours not very easy to negotiate, palms and cockatoos,
and a people, a race of men and women, childlike—savages if
you like, for they fought each other with poisoned arrows, and
quite often were cannibals—at the same time curiously attractive
and, unless maltreated by traders, approachable and confiding.
Well, he was their father in God, and he had made several
voyages already, exploring this strange charge, landing unarmed
before the possibility of a shower of arrows. And he had brought
away a handful of boys to be trained, and to teach their teachers
the language or languages, for there was nothing so simple as a
tongue shared by all the islanders. He was sure that this method
was the right one, but it needed a heaven-sent linguist to make it
work, and Selwyn had New Zealand, with its White and Maori
problems to care for, and couldn't, however much it fascinated
him, give the time needed to the Melanesian people. Some other
Christian bodies had experimented in some of the islands, but
most of them were virgin ground. Well, the Lord did provide.

Here was a young man who had lapped up Hebrew and Arabic, and obviously had gifts as a linguist; he had character enough to be a leader of men, and what the Bishop liked especially, a really warm heart. In his short ministry at Alfington he had knitted the people to him, and embraced them in a way that showed Selwyn that he knew about the Love of God. This Coleridge stock, as he knew from the quality of his remarkable wife, was religious to the core. So in the end it was settled; Coleridge Patteson was to go with Selwyn in the new year to this venturesome work.

We must look back a little at the family setting of this young deacon. His father had been made a judge at the early age of forty, and had a great reputation among the men of his own profession. He was also a man very firm in his faith, very charitable and kind. He married twice, and his second marriage brought him into the Coleridge cousinhood, into a great family circle of fine people. He had a daughter, Joan, by his first marriage, and Fanny, John Coleridge and Jem, by his second one. It was a deeply affectionate family, and when the mother died while the boys were still at school, the father became the centre of their affections, and his principles and his faith played a great part in forming their values.

The Judge had been a colleger at Eton, and Coley was sent there to the House of an uncle of his. His Eton career had been striking. It was a scholarly career, his work was 'sent up for good' as many as twenty-seven times: but it had also been remarkable in other ways. He had the moral courage to stand out against any talk or habit that offended his family standards. He and three of his friends used to meet and read the Bible in his room, with a drawer open to receive the Bible, and a Shakespeare open above it, in case they were raided. He was also one of the best cricketers in the school, and had some brilliant moments at Lord's. Coley adored Eton; somehow it never lost its hold on him. He used to go back there from Oxford, and once wrote to his father: 'I think if one was to look out simply for one's own selfish pleasure in this world, staying at Eton in the summer is Paradise. I cetainly have not been so happy for years, and they need no convincing there of my doting attachment to the place.'

Oxford, even Balliol in the 1840's, seemed rather an anticlimax. It isn't clear when he decided to be ordained, but it was probably early in his Oxford years. One of his friends there, Principal Shairp, wrote of him:

> Patteson as he was at Oxford, comes back to me as the representative of the very best kind of Etonian. . . . I remember well the look he had then; his countenance was massive for one so young, with good sense and good feeling, in fact full of character. For it was character, more than special ability which marked him out from others, and made him wherever he was, whether in cricket in which he excelled, or in graver things, a centre round which others gathered. . . . We did not know, probably he did not know himself, the fire of devotion that lay within him, but that was soon to kindle and make him what he afterwards became.

At Oxford, he somehow escaped the bitterness of the controversies that were still raging. Pusey was his cousin, and from his upbringing he would inherit a sort of sober Tractarianism. After hearing Pusey's sermon on absolution he wrote home: 'He preached the doctrine to my mind in an invincible manner. His immense benevolence beams through the extreme power of his argument . . . as for the humility and prayerful spirit in which it was composed, you fancied he must have been on his knees all the time he was writing it.'

In 1849 he got a second class, and though he meant to return
to Oxford and try for a Fellowship, he made a break in his life
with some long visits to Europe. This was important in two
ways; first he discovered his aptitude, almost amounting to
genius, for learning languages, and for the study of philology;
and then the pictures, the mountains, and the music got under
his skin, and he grew enormously in his appreciation of what
was beautiful. When the long parting from all this came, it is
one of the parts of his sacrifice that must be reckoned with. In
those days one could not put a record on to a gramophone
and reproductions of good pictures were scarce and not very
good. He wrote to his sister of the great pictures in Rome and
Florence: 'None can see them and be unchanged. I never had
such enjoyment.'

It was in 1852 after a year or two of work abroad, studying
German, Hebrew and Arabic in Dresden and elsewhere, that he
stood for, and obtained a Fellowship of Merton. He went
straight from Dresden to Oxford without coming home, and a
letter to his sister Joan, telling her of this plan, gives one a sudden
insight into what it would mean for him later to go so far away
from the dear family atmosphere: 'It is a long time to pass without seeing you all. I have not grown out of an occasional fit of
homesickness yet, and at these times Arthur and I talk inces-
santly about domestic matters, and indulge our fancies with
what you are all doing, and so forth. How I remember every
inch of the dear old places.' Friends at Oxford noticed how much
he had developed in those years abroad and one of them wrote
later: 'The moral and spiritual forces of the man were now
vivified, refined, and strengthened by the awaking of his intellectual and aesthetic nature.'

He had a considerable amount of influence on the policies of

34

his college. University reform was rather an unfashionable thing. 'He threw himself into the work with hearty zeal; and supported every liberal proposal. To his loyal fidelity and common sense is largely due the success with which the reform of Merton was carried out.' So wrote a contemporary. Patteson stayed at Merton till 1853. He retained his Fellowship until his death, and with it many Oxford friendships.

Coleridge's cousin Charlotte Yonge, who wrote his life, gives us a very good picture of his appearance at this date.

> He was tall, and of a large powerful frame, broad in the chest and shoulders, and with small neat hands and feet, with more of sheer muscular strength and power of endurance than healthiness. His complexion was very dark, and there was a strongly marked line between the cheek and mouth. The most striking feature were his eyes, which were of a very dark clear blue. . . . His smile was remarkably bright, sweet and affectionate, like a gleam of sunshine, and was one element in his great attractiveness. So was his voice which had the rich full sweetness inherited from his mother's family, which always exercised a winning influence over his hearers. Thus though not a handsome man, he was more than commonly engaging, exciting the warmest affection in all who were concerned with him, and giving in return an immense amount of interest and sympathy.

He was such a home person, and there was such a loving family and cousinhood all round, that to let him go to the other side of the world was a tremendous giving for all of them. Selwyn had not minimized the dangers of the new venture, and it must have entered into the minds of all who loved him to wonder how this sensitive endearing young man would endure the loneliness and hardship of his chosen life. He was ordained priest at Michaelmas 1854, and Selwyn meant to sail in their own little vessel, the 'Southern Cross', in the New Year, though in the end, they sailed in another ship. Meanwhile he went quietly on with his work at Alfington, where his indignant congregation accused the Bishop of having stolen away the parson they loved so much. He wrote to his cousin Arthur Coleridge: 'I am almost strangely free from excitement. I live on exactly as I did before, and even when alone with Father, talk just as I used to talk, have nothing more to tell him, not knowing how to make a better use of these last quiet evenings.' The Judge said quite firmly that Coley must never feel bound to come home if illness should overtake his father. There seemed to be a feeling in the family that this might be a final parting, unless one reads into their words the end that was to come. Coley, writing to a very old friend, Miss Neill, who had been governess to the Pattesons said:

> There will be seasons of loneliness and sadness, and it seems to me as if it always was so in the case of all the people we read of in the Bible. Our Lord distinctly told His disciples to expect it to be so, and even experienced this sorrow of heart Himself . . . so I don't learn that I ought exactly to wish it to be otherwise, so much is said in the Bible about being partakers of His sufferings; only I pray that it may please God to bear me up in the midst of it.

This same friend had given him a cross, and after he has told her that he is wearing it round his neck, he writes: 'May God grant that I may wear your precious gift not only *on* but *in* my heart.' There were still some joys which remained delightful memories always. The people at Alfington had all subscribed to give him a Bible at Christmas, and he loved their gift. And then unexpectedly there was a wonderful week's skating (the last time that he ever trod ice), a large merry party of cousins all skating together, little boys scrambling for nuts, and finally a wetting through venturing onto thin ice. But at last the day came, and he walked down alone to catch the coach, stopping for a moment in the churchyard to pick some primrose buds from his mother's grave.

His uncle, who saw him on to his ship, wrote to his father: 'I never saw a hand set on the plough with more firmness, yet entire modesty, or with an eye and heart less turned backwards on the world behind.'

We have in these last years read and heard so much about the South Sea Islands that it is hard to imagine how strange and new they were to the Victorian bishop and the young priest who were to explore them for Christ. One thing links Coley to the enchanting writer of *A Pattern of Islands*. Both found the South Sea Islander a fascinating and companionable person. The group of Islands where Patteson was to work were farther south than the Gilbert Islands, and the islanders were Melanesians, not Polynesians, a taller darker-skinned race. Bishop Selwyn, anxious not to intrude where other Christian bodies were at work, left the Polynesian folk to the London Missionary Society, and himself concentrated on the more southerly New Hebrides, Banks, and Loyalty Islands which were nearer to his New Zealand Diocese.

Patteson's first companions in the southern hemisphere were Maories, studying at Auckland in St John's College. But the arrival of the new ship, the 'Southern Cross', was the signal for his first voyage with Selwyn among the islands. He had proved himelf apt to learn navigation, and had already shown his strange proficiency as a linguist by picking up much of the Maori tongue. They had come through some bad weather on the voyage out, and he had not been dismayed. It seemed to Bishop Selwyn that his young priest was shaping well as a messenger to the Islands. Both men had a hilarious morning rather to Patteson's surprise in having what he calls a 'mudlark', landing stuff from the 'Southern Cross', which had proved itself on the voyage out to be a seaworthy little ship. All was set for the next step. He got into the feel of the new ship in two short voyages to Wellington, when he carried two passengers who afterwards became his greatest friends: Judge Martin, a fellow-student of languages, and his wife. The ship was now to be his home, and in a letter to Miss Neill he writes:

> My home is the 'Southern Cross', where I live always, in harbour as at sea . . . highly contented with the possession of a cosy little cabin, nicely furnished with table, lots of books, and my father's photograph. . . . In harbour I live in the cabin. It is hung round with barometers, sympiesometers, fixed chest for chronometers, charts, etc. I am the most complete skipper. I feel as natural with my quadrant in my hand as of old with a cricket bat.

His first voyage with Selwyn in the 'Southern Cross' was a mixed bag of experience. First came a journey to Sydney to try to arrange that Norfolk Island, where the climate was more suited to the New Hebrides boys than the climate of Auckland, should be the training centre for the Melanesian boys. But Norfolk Island had just been alloted to the Pitcairn Islanders, and the Australian government, who did not approve of a mixture of interests there, refused their request. Then began the voyage proper among the islands. Their first stop, to deliver mail, was at a flourishing mission belonging to the Presbyterian Church, all in very correct mission station order, giving Patteson a glimpse of what he always longed for, a long stay on one island.

They went on almost at once from there to their own objective the New Hebrides, and came first to Faté, which had a bad reputation for cannibalism, where they made no landing, but where Coley saw his first Melanesians in their natural state. The

'Southern Cross' was soon surrounded by men in canoes. Girdles of beautifully plaited coco-nut fibre were their only clothing, but some had wreaths of flowers and green leaves round their heads. Two of the young men stayed aboard, being willing to go with the white men, and teach them their language. Patteson was soon picking up words with an almost uncanny facility, and buttoning the men into shirts in true Victorian style and having his first taste of sleeping with islanders in his room. 'Our Faté friends being presented each with a blanket, just wound themselves up on the cabin floor, close to Leonard and me, and slept away in style.'

The ship went on to Espiritu Santo, and to Malicolo, where they had a clash with a brig, raiding for labour, of the kind which later caused so much suspicion and trouble among the islanders.

Two things became clear to Coley on this first voyage. He was going to love the Melanesians, especially the children and boys, and they were going to like him; and he was going to find the Islands exquisitely beautiful. Here he has landed:

There was no shyness on the part of the children, dear little fellows from six to ten, clustering round me, unable to understand my coat with pockets, and what my socks could be. I seemed to have two or three skins! A Negone man was ashore, and with him I could talk a little. Soon I was walking on shore, arm in arm with him, stark naked, a little boy of the island held the other hand, and so leaving the boat we walked inland to see a native village . . . spears I saw none, but bows and arrows. I took a bow out of a man's hand, and then an arrow, and fitted it to the string. He made signs that he shot birds with it. There is a good deal of fighting on the island however. But there is every indication of friendliness and of a gentle and soft disposition. I never saw children more thoroughly attractive in appearance and manner.

39

Oh, the beauty of the deep clefts in the coral reef, lined coral, purple, blue, scarlet, green and white . . . the little blue fishes, the bright blue star fish, the little land crabs, walking away with other people's shells!

Oh, the wonerful beauty of the scene, sea and river alike, fringed with the richest foliage, birds flying about (I saw a large blue bird, parrot I suppose) fish jumping, the perfectly still water, the mysterious smoke of a fire or two, the call of a man heard in the bush; just enough of novelty to quicken me to full enjoyment of such a lovely bay as no English eyes save ours have ever seen.

On the other hand, a ridgeway of a house hung with skulls, and traces of a cannibal orgy on another island, were reminders of ominous things which no beauty could really discount. After this first enterprise Coley and the Bishop took the 'Southern Cross' back to St John, with their little cargo of boys and young men who were going to teach and learn, and Coley began the teaching part of his apprenticeship.

My occupation most interesting, working away with the twelve Melanesians at languages, etc., with the highest of all incentives to perseverance, trying to form in them habits of cleanliness, order, decency.

Last night, their first Sunday in New Zealand, after explaining to the Solomon Island's boys, seven in number, the nature of the Lord's Prayer, as far as my knowledge of their language would carry me, I thought myself justified in making them kneel round me, and they uttered with their lips, after me, the first words of prayer to their Father in Heaven. I don't venture to say that they understood much—neither does the young child, taught at his mother's knee, neither do many grown-up people perhaps know much about the fullness of the prayer of prayers. These scenes teach me my ignorance which is one great gain. . . . Yet they knew, I think, that they were praying to some great and mighty one—not an abstraction—a conscious loving Being, a Father, and they know at least the name of His Son Jesus Christ.

But they didn't thrive too well, these tropical children, suddenly transplanted to a temperate climate. It was too cold for them at St Johns, and they had to wear clothes to stand up to the cold, and to learn to live in clothes was not particularly easy. But Coley, so the Bishop wrote to his father, had conquered all fastidiousness in his care for them. 'The four youngest, sixteen to eighteen, sleep in my room. One is now on my bed, wrapped up in a great oppossum rug, with cold and slight fever. . . . I have to watch over them like a cat.'

He was picking up their language with astounding quickness, and writes to Miss Neill:

I talk to them about common things, and learn a great deal about their weird savage customs, but I can do little yet in the way of real instruction. Some ideas I trust they are beginning to acquire concerning our Blessed Lord. If it come to pass that for some years I can retain a hold of them, they may be instructed sufficiently to make them teachers in their turn to their own people. But all this is in the Hands of God. Don't believe in the ferocity of the islanders. When their passions are excited they do commit fearful deeds, and they are almost universally cannibals; after a battle there will nearly always be a cannibal feast—not otherwise. But treat them well and prudently, and I apprehend that there is little danger in visiting them, meaning by visiting merely landing on the beach the first time, going perhaps to a native village the next time, sleeping on shore the third, spending ten days or so, the fourth.

He may have been a little too careless, as Charlotte Yonge records that the Bishop sometimes had to give him a sharp warning to be on the alert and not to loiter. But at the moment he was in the first flush of his missionary vision. Here he is writing to his uncle the Eton Housemaster after his second voyage:

I wouldn't exchange my position with these lads and young men
for anything. I wish you could see them and know them . . . it is
no effort to love them heartily. My love is most poured out on my
Bauro and Gera lads. They are such dear fellows, and I trust that
already they begin to know something about religion. . . . I have
quite learnt to believe that there are no savages anywhere, at least
among black and coloured people. I'd like to see anyone call my
Bauro boys savages! Why, the fellows on the reef that have never
seen a white man, will wade back to the boat, and catch one's arm
to prevent one falling into pits among the coral, just like an old
nurse looking after a child. This they did at Santa Maria where we
two swam ashore to a party of forty or fifty men, and where our
visit was evidently an agreeable one on both sides, though we
didn't know one syllable of the language then.

There were moments which must have seemed more grim, as
when they walked on one island into an empty space, with four
hollowed trunks of trees surrounding two great stones, the trees
carved into the likeness of grotesque human heads, and among
them a sort of temple made of sloping bamboos and pandanus
leaves from whence hung a dead man, with his face painted in
stripes of red and yellow. And Coley didn't know enough of
the language to find out the why or wherefore of this.

They began to go to places where Bishop Selwyn had not
penetrated before, and Coley wrote: 'We get into the habit of
landing among strangers, the knack of managing with signs,
and gesticulations, and the feeling of ease and confidence which
engenders confidence and good will in others.' Patteson in these
first voyages had not seen the fearful deaths from tetanus which
were the results of even a scratch from the deadly little arrows,
and there were quite enough bows and arrows in the hands of
wondering islanders to make each landing a considerable adventure. But he writes lightheartedly and perhaps a little incon-

siderately to his sisters at home: 'You would have liked to see me standing on a rock with my two supporters, two fine young men who will I trust go with us next time, my arms round their necks, and a fine background of some thirty or forty dark figures with bows and arrows.'

When they reached an island which had been visited before, Coley went to spend the night in the house of the Chief Iri, in a big hut partly divided by a screen of bamboo: 'Iri and his wife and an orphan girl slept on one side of the screen, and the two lads slept on my side of it. I can't say I slept at all for the rats were so very many—coming in through the bamboos on every side.' But he sent one of the lads for water and shaved the next morning to the great admiration of Iri and the ladies. He spent a Sunday visiting on the island and having long talks: 'a sort of half preaching, half conversing these talks were' and the old chief reported, 'He said we were not like dogs and pigs, or birds or fishes, because these cannot speak or think, they all die and no one knows anything more about them, but he say we shall not die like that, but rise up again.'

Selwyn and Patteson were involved in an intensely difficult bit of missionary strategy, and one wonders as one reads of the flourishing Melanesian Mission of the present day, to see how it grew from their scattered beginnings. Coley wrote home that they were in touch with seventy-four different islands. It was a sound plan that Bishop Selwyn had evolved to take some boys and young men away from the islands to a school where they could learn enough of the Christian faith to begin to introduce it to their fellow-islanders. But he had failed hitherto to find a place for such a school where the children of the tropics could thrive. Auckland was too cold, and a sheltered bay to the north was tried for a time, but Patteson's next experiment was

on an island, Lifu, in the Loyalty group which had lost its
L.M.S. staff, and where he hoped to collect boys in the summer
until L.M.S. could send more workers. There were buildings
that he could use, and some sort of foundations of goodwill had
been laid, and there was a young, friendly chief. It was hard
going. He had twelve scholars speaking six different languages,
and he found himself strangely incompetent in practical ways.
No Scout movement had taught the young Etonians of his day
to cook and carpenter, and to render first aid. There had always
been tradesmen, servants, and doctors available in the Victorian
home.

> I can hardly tell you, (he wrote home) how much I regret not
> knowing something about the treatment of simple surgical cases.
> I am now in a position to know what to learn were I once more in
> England, to spend one day a week with old Fry, the mason, and
> another with John Venn, the carpenter, and two every week at the
> Exeter Hospital. Every Missionary ought to be a carpenter, mason,
> something of a butcher and a good deal of a cook.

Still he was superb at his own skills. He had landed in Lifu in
mid June, and by the first day of August he was preaching in
what had been an unknown language. He had no white fellow-
worker, and it was no help when an irate French priest turned up
to claim that the island was in the French sphere of New Caledonia. He was beginning to see that much more difficult than
the actual teaching in words was the building up of a Christian
community. 'True, they don't fight so much, or eat each other
now, but, beyond that, are they elevated as men? The same diet,
the same houses, the same idle vicious habits, in most cases no
sense of decency or very little. Where is the expression of Scrip-
tural life?' And he very wisely puts the emphasis where he sees
it: 'For lack of connecting Christian teaching with the improve-

ment in social life, in hut or village, which is the necessary corollary and complement of such teaching.'

He had expected Bishop Selwyn and the 'Southern Cross' at the beginning of September; his stores were running out, and he had nothing but the native food which didn't always agree with him; the coffee and biscuit that he allowed himself, being used up. But at last the ship came, and he and Selwyn went on picking up recruits for the Winter School from various islands, and returning with a company of sixty-three Melanesians. As very often happened he was sharing accommodation with his scarcely house-trained boys. The Bishop had charge of the ladies for whom part of the cabin had been screened off: 'One gets so used to this sort of thing' (he writes lightly) 'that I sleep just as well as I used to in my own bed at home.'

Now they had their eyes on another island that they had visited, as a possible training home, though they both felt that some of the training must be in New Zealand. At Vanua Lava, Patteson had found a people

most simple gentle and docile, unwarlike, not cannibals; I verily believe as good a specimen of natural fallen man as can be met with, wholly naked yet with no sense of shame in consequence, timid, yet soon learning to confide in one, intelligent, and gleaming with plenty of spirit and fun. So I hope (he ends) that we may get a missionary for Lifu, and I may be free to spend all my time, when not in New Zealand, at Vanua Lava.

When he got home to Auckland he had the great pleasure of finding Judge and Mrs Martin, who had been home to England, and had visited his own people at Feniton, and spent some time with his father and sisters. These congenial friends joined the party at St John's College which now consisted of 40 Melanesians, two printers, and a volunteer helper, Mr Dudley, who later

45

went with Patteson to the Islands. 'Not a little happy', he exclaims, 'I feel at the head of my board with two rows of merry, happy-looking Melanesians on either side of me!' Mrs Martin found him still more deeply absorbed in his work.

> He was always ready to listen to anything there was to tell about his father—but about our foreign travels, his favourite pictures, the scenes of which we had heard so much from him, he would listen for a few minutes, but was sure in a little while to have worked round to Melanesia in general and to his boys in particular, or to some discussion with my husband on the structure of their many languages and dialects.

After the hardships of his beds on the floor, he had comfortable quarters in one long room at St John's, but Mrs Martin tells that there was always some sick lad there, wrapped up in his best rugs in the warmest nook by the fire. She felt that he was not at his happiest teaching in class, but:

> Every person in the place loved to come to evening classes in his own room, where in their own language he opened to them the Scriptures, and spoke to them of the Kingdom of God. It was in these private classes that he exercised such wonderful influence; his musical voice, his holy face, his gentle manner, all helping doubtless to impress and draw even the dullest. Long after this he told me how after the evening classes, one by one, some young fellow or small boy would come back with a gentle tap at the door, 'I want to talk to you', and then and there the heart would be laid open, and counsel asked of the beloved teacher.

He was longing for more helpers, but they must be of the right kind; he was ahead of his time in what he demanded:

> Men sent out as clergymen to the Mission field who would not have been thought fit to receive Holy Orders at home are not at all the men we want. It is not at all probable that such men would

46

understand the natives, love them, and live with them; but they would be great dons, keeping the natives at a distance, assuming that they could have little in common, ideas wholly destructive of success in Missionary or other work. The pride of race which prompts a white man to regard coloured people as inferior to himself is strongly ingrained in most men's minds, and must be wholly eradicated before they will ever win hearts and thus the souls of the heathen.

Just at this time the question of a furlough for him arose. His father was content for him not to come home, but other friends wrote from England, urging a holiday and a visit to England. Probably it would have been well for him to go before his office as a bishop made it almost impossible to leave; but he was sure himself that he ought not to go home, though he knew the cost of this decision. He was committed to Melanesia in a way that brooked no turning back even for a time.

> I see nothing at all to make it likely that I shall ever revisit England. I can't very well conceive any such state of things as would make it my duty to gratify my constant inclination. And, my dear father, I don't scruple to say that I am happier here than I should be in England, where even though I were absent only a few months, I should bear about with me the constant weight of knowing that Melanesia was not provided for.

But it was his 'constant inclination'. He and the Bishop had their last joint expedition that year among the islands, finding a great welcome in most of them, though by now white traders were beginning to create a prejudice in some of the islands against the white man. On this voyage we hear for the first time of Nukapu, an island to the north of the Santa Cruz group, easily raided by ships from Fiji.

Selwyn was sure now that Melanesia could not be worked by a bishop, with as much on his hands as the Bishop of New

Zealand must have. There must be a Bishop of Melanesia, and who more suitable than this man whom God had given to him? He began about this time to propose this to Patteson, and to get leave from England to make the appointment. Patteson was not one to accept the office of a bishop without a preliminary recoil, for he was above all things humble. It was not the work or the responsibility that outfaced him, but a doubt of his own spiritual fitness. He understood the spiritual power that would be needed to withstand the assaults of the devil in his beloved islands. He had seen how far his children had to go to build the Church in Melanesia. He wrote to his father:

> I do feel frightened when I see that I do not become more prayer-ful, more real in communion with God. That is what I must pray for, to become more prayerful, more constantly impressed with the necessity of seeking everything from Him. Now it is coming to this—a Church to be planted, organized, edified among the wild heathen inhabitants of Melanesia, and what hope can there be for me if there is no growth of a thankful humble spirit of prayer and love and adoration.

He was himself absolutely willing to work under any man who should be sent out as Bishop; but to Selwyn who had watched him for six years, he seemed the man who had courage enough, and love enough to plant the Church in the lovely, dangerous, unknown islands. They had decided to move their school in New Zealand to a more sheltered site than the old windswept St John's. At Kohimarama in the new or transferred buildings Coley felt himself very much delighted with the youngest of his batch of new boys. 'I have the jolliest little fellows this time, about seven of them, fellows scarcely too big to take on my knee and talk to about God, Heaven, and Jesus Christ; and I feel almost as if I had an instinct of love towards

48

them as they look up wondering with their deep, deep eyes, and ask their simple questions.'

It was in this autumn that his father wrote to tell him that his doctors did not expect him to live long. It was a strong peaceful letter, the father quite realizing that he was not going to see his son again, and committing him to his work with much love and patience. It meant a good deal of hidden anguish to this son who loved his father with such longing dependence on his constant interest and concern. Some of this he confided to his New Zealand friend Dudley who wrote of him at this time: 'It was the anguish he endured as night after night he lay awake thinking of his father, gradually sinking and craving for him, and cheerfully resigning him, that really told upon him. I know I obtained then a glimpse of an affection and a depth of sorrow such as perfectly awed me.'

In that summer of 1860 Patteson took Dudley, who turned out to be a man of his hands, for his companion. He was able to give really efficient help, when they built the first church premises in Melanesia on Mota Island in the Banks Islands group, among friendly people who had not been disturbed by traders. It was the Mota dialect which Patteson chose for his translations of the Bible. The building was fairly primitive, some planks that they had brought from Auckland being used for the flooring and the roof being made native-wise with palm leaves: the furniture consisted of four boxes which became tables, desks, and chairs in turn. Beds there were none, but the planks brought from Auckland at least secured a level floor. 'We all had something level to lie on at night', wrote Coley, 'and when you are tired enough a good smooth plank does as well as a mattress.' Some land was actually acquired by the Mission, the chiefs making their mark, though Coley rather laughed at his amateur conveyancing. He came up against what must have been initiation ceremonies for the boys, and was afraid that they would not be allowed to come to his hut, but though they went away for a time, they did come back. One of his embarrassments was that the islanders on one side of the island would try to defend him from those on the other. 'He always had such an attraction for them that they would throng around him eagerly wherever he went', wrote Dudley. St Barnabas' day that year was marked by their first Communion service on Melanesian soil; some of the boys who had been training at St Johns making their first Communion.

That summer saw the end of their beloved little ship the 'Southern Cross', which struck a rock, and broke up, and when after a long hungry wait a ship came to take them off, it was the clumsy old schooner 'Zillah', all that Bishop Selwyn had been able to get hold of, and not planned to accommodate the Mission.

When he got back to New Zealand, Patteson found that his consecration was nearer than he expected, and that bishops from Australia were coming to assist in it, early in 1861; St Matthias day being finally fixed for it. He was now looking ahead to his future work and to doing without Selwyn's constant leadership:

> I feel now the sense of responsibility is deepening on me, I must go out to work without him, and very anxious I am sometimes, and almost oppressed by it. But strength will come, and it is not one's own work, which is a comfort, and if I fail—which is very likely— God will place some other man in my position, and the work will go on, whether in my hands or not, and that is the real point.
>
> Indeed I do wonder that I am calm (he writes later) when one moment's look at the map or thought of the countless islands quite overwhelms me. How to get at them? Where to begin? How to decide on the best method of teaching? But I must try to be

patient, and to be content with very small beginnings, and endings too, perhaps.

There were many moving moments at his consecration. He was so far away from the loving family, who would, of course, have been present had he been consecrated in England. One thing that helped him very much was a little service on the Eve of St Matthias.

> Yesterday, at 6 p.m. in the little chapel at Tararina, the three bishops, the dear Judge, Lady Martin, Mrs Abraham, Mr Lloyd and I met for special prayer. How we missed Mrs Selwyn from amongst us, and how my thoughts passed on to you.
>
> Evening hymn, Exhortation in the Consecration service, Litany from the St Augustine's Missionary Manual, with the questions in the Consecration service turned into prayers, Ps 132, 131 and 51, special prayer for the elect Bishop among the heathen, and the Gloria in Excelsis. Then the Bishop walked over to me, and taking my hand in both his, looking at me with that smile of deep love, and deep, deep thought, so seldom seen, and so deeply prized: 'I can't tell you what I feel', he said in a low broken voice, 'You know it—my heart is too full.' . . . and so we both stood with tears in our eyes, and I unable to speak.

Mrs Abraham records that he had ten of his island boys close to him at his consecration, one of them Tagalana, kneeling behind him, held the book for the Primate to read from at the imposition of hands. Lady Martin wrote: 'I shall never forget the expression of his face . . . it was meek, holy and calm, as though all the conflict were over and he was resting in Divine strength.' The Bishop of Wellington writing home to a friend said: 'Perhaps the most marked feature of his character is his genuine simplicity and humility. I never saw it equalled in one so gifted, honoured, and beloved. . . . Certainly he is the most perfect character I ever met.' Coley's thoughts after the service were with the islands, especially the ones he hardly knew:

> How I think of those islands, how I see those bright coral and sandy beaches . . . hundreds of people are crowding upon them, naked, armed, with wild uncouth cries and gestures, I cannot talk to them but by signs. But they are my children now. . . . I have now, as I write, a deepening sense of what the charge must be that has passed over to me. Again I go, by God's blessing, for seven months to Melanesia.

At the moment he had no helpers except Dudley and Pritt. Pritt had done a lot of practical work at Kohimarama, and there was a little farm connected with the school. He found this useful from the teaching point of view in stressing reliability, regularity and neatness. He had no ship of his own this season and went on his voyage in a gunboat lent by the government. As there was now the rough building on Mota, he left Dudley and Pritt there to develop what he had started.

All this summer was clouded by the knowledge that his father's death was not far away. The old man had lived to hear all the news about the consecration, but Coley knew that on his return from his voyage he might find news of his father's death. In a wonderful way he had held on to a sense of companionship with his father on the other side of the world. 'How I did delight in writing to him', he confessed to his uncle, 'and in seeking his approval of what I was about'.

He knew that his own life was constantly in danger. 'I have some islands to visit in this next month or two' (he wrote home), 'where the people are very wild.' It was always a horridly responsible decision, 'whether or not I ought to lower a boat in such a seaway, whether or not I ought to swim ashore among these fellows crowded on the narrow beach.' He acquired a helper on this voyage who afterwards became the skipper of his new 'Southern Cross'. Captain Tilley was a faithful friend, and was with him till his death.

Calling at Norfolk Island to talk to two young men Fisher Young, and Edwin Nobbs, who had volunteered to serve with him, he heard of his father's death. It was mentioned almost casually by the Norfolk Island people, who had seen it in the papers. 'I showed by my face that I had not known before that God had taken him, but I could answer quite calmly, "I thank God we all knew that he was only waiting for Christ"'. Dudley wrote:

> He took it quite calmly, evidently it had been expected and pre-pared for. In the evening there was singing got up for him by some of the Norfolk Islanders. He enjoyed it, and after it had gone on sometime he thanked them in a few touching words that went home, I am sure, to the hearts of many of them, and then we all knelt down, and he prayed extempore. I wish I had kept the word of that prayer.

It cheered him to think that the parents of Fisher Young and Edward Nobbs were offering their sons as his own father had offered him. He saw in these two young men the sort of worker that he wanted to train. Nobbs was the son of the parson who cared for the Pitcairn folk. Fisher also was of the Pitcairn stock.

The main winter quarters were still at Kohimarama, and here he returned from this rather shorter voyage in 1861. Lady Martin wrote at this time: 'The great charm of the place was the freedom and naturalness of the whole party. The Bishop had not lost his Eton tastes, and liked to see them play games, and the little, fat merry-faced boys were always on the look out for a bit of fun with him.' So he worked away with them through the winter, and chartered a schooner, 'Sea Breeze', in which to make his

1862 voyage. This was a wonderful voyage, so different from the tragic ones that followed, a sort of halcyon adventure, of which Patteson wrote to his uncle:

> I never recollect myself so remarkable a voyage as this last. . . . It pleased God to prosper us beyond our utmost hopes. I was not only able to land in many places where, as far as I know, no white man had ever set foot before, but to go inland, to inspect the houses, canoes, etc., in crowded villages as at Santa Cruz, or to sit for two hours alone among a crowd of people, or to walk two and a half miles inland . . . fifty-one Melanesian men, women, and lads are now with us, gathered from twenty-four islands. . . . Throughout this voyage, during which I landed between seventy or eighty times, not one hand was lifted up against me, not one sign of ill-will exhibited.

Some of these Melanesian passengers he left at Mota, but he still had twenty-one, speaking eleven different languages.

There had been a partly formed plan that his sisters, Joan and Fan, should come out to visit him in the winter months at Kohimarana; but in the end he felt that life even there would not suit them, and that he could not see enough of them to justify the long voyage without neglecting his work.

He was concerning himself with possible recruits from England, and wrote to his cousin Derwent Coleridge, principal of St Mark's training college, Chelsea:

> I'm not in a hurry for men, but I should be thankful by and by to have men equally willing to do anything, yet better educated than my Norfolk Island boys in respect of book knowledge. Earnest, bright, cheerful fellows, without that notion of making sacrifices, etc., perpetually occurring to their minds, would be invaluable. . . . A man who takes a sentimental view of coral islands and coco-nuts of course is worse than useless, a man possessed with the idea of making sacrifices will never do; and a man who thinks any kind of work 'beneath a gentleman' will be simply in the way,

and be rather uncomfortable to see his Bishop do what he thinks degrading to himself.

He got two new workers from New Zealand, Joe Atkin, and John Palmer, a theological student at St Johns. Dudley, however, went home for health's sake after his marriage. The new 'Southern Cross' arrived in February ready for the next summer's voyage. Charlotte Yonge had paid for much of it from her royalties on the *Daisy Chain*, and he wrote to her: 'What it is to us even you can hardly tell. I know not how to pour out my thankfulness.'

Keble got a letter, too, thanking him for his part in the gift, and asking for prayers for the boys and himself. 'We are their teachers, the only representatives of Christianity among them. How inexpressibly solemn and fearful. This is the thought so perpetually present to me.'

But before the sailing time came they had a terrible outbreak of dysentry at Kohimarama. It fell on the Melanesians most heavily and some of them died. Fortunately they were still in New Zealand, and friends rallied round, and there were doctors to be had. One of these friends wrote of Patteson: 'I can find no words to describe the devotion with which the Bishop nursed his boys, comforting them, and supporting them, never shrinking from the most repulsive offices, even bearing the dead out silently at night, lest the others should see and be alarmed.' Six of his boys died; as he knelt by the body of the last one in the chapel, he found thankfully that he could still praise and bless God in his heart. But the friend adds: 'I wonder if I ever went through such acute mental suffereing, but now the brightness seems to be coming back.'

The new little ship sailed on May the 22nd, and Mr Codrington, a young clergyman who had been a Fellow of Wadham, came for a trial trip. It was good for Coley to have his company, and he was also finding great support in the Master of his ship, Captain Tilley. Tilley had taken to Patteson ever since he came aboard the ship drenched from launching his boat through the surf at Kohimarama, and 'Seemed more like a sailor than a clergyman'. He gives an unforgettable picture of Patteson paying a visit to a new island.

> We pulled into a small inner islet among a group where a company of say 200 natives were gathered on the beach. Seeing they looked as if friendly, he waded on shore without hesitation and joined them; the reception was friendly, and after a while he walked with them along the beach, we in the boat keeping near. After a time we took him into the boat again, and lay off the beach a few yards to be clear of the throng and to be able to get at the things he wanted to give them, they coming about the boats in canoes; and this is the fact I want to notice, viz. the look on his face while the intercourse between them lasted. I was so struck with it quite involuntary, as I had no idea of watching for anything of the sort; but it was one of such extreme gentleness, and of yearning towards them.

It was a cheering voyage though not a very long one, and he wrote to Derwent Coleridge:

> I see everywhere signs of a change really extraordinary in the last few years. . . . I know that in twenty or thirty or perhaps forty places where a year or so ago, no white man could land without some little uncertainty as to his reception, I can feel confident now of meeting with friends. I can walk inland, a thing never dreamt of in old days, sleep ashore, and put myself entirely in their hands and meet with a return of confidence on their part.

In fact the powers of evil were getting rather worried about Melanesia; one can imagine a very tart letter from Screwtape on the subject. They braced themselves for action.

But first Patteson had an interesting interlude in Australia. The Australian churches were beginning to bear some of the expense of the Island Diocese, and they invited Patteson to come to their synod and to preach in various centres. It was a change, and rather good for him to find himself in a luxurious cabin 'lounging about' on red velvet sofas and cushions. His preaching had a startling effect on the Australians, and he himself felt a great release of power. 'There were times', he wrote to Fan, 'when I lost all sense of nervousness and self, and only wished there were 10,000 people present, for I felt that I was speaking out face to face simple words of truth.'

The Dean of Melbourne said publicly that 'No such earnestness in religious matters had ever been exhibited there.'

Coley wrote to Fan:

It was a sight to see St George's Hall crowded. . . . Now you know my old vanity, thank God I don't think it followed me here. There was a strong sense of a grand opportunity, and the need of grace to use it. I had to preach extempore for the most part. I didn't like it, but what could I do? Sermons and speeches followed like hail. Now, old Fan, you know the misery of self-consciousness and conceit clings to me. I can't as dear old Father could, tell you what actually occurred without doing myself harm. It pleased God to make me say all through what I think was good for people to hear.

It was as well that he had this interlude to prepare him for the voyage of 1864. Even in its early stages, Patteson was threatened by a man with a club. He sat still till two other Melanesians pulled off his assailant. Then there was an affair about buying yams, when the islanders fought over the division of hatchets used as payment and there were arrows shot all round them. On that occasion 'I was thankful to get well out of it', said Coley.

And then they came to Santa Cruz. All seemed to be going well and Patteson was keen to renew his links with these people whom he had not visited for three years. He took his five young men with him in the boat, Fisher Young, Nobbs, Adkin, Hunt Christian, and Pearce, and made two or three good landings, stayed awhile at a native house and came back to the boat. Then suddenly for no reason that he could see, the people on the reef began to shoot at them. He had not shipped the rudder, and held it up hoping to use it as a shield for the young men in the boat, but before they got to the ship three had received deadly arrow wounds as the canoes chased them to the schooner. They treated the arrow wounds as best they could; all the young men behaved with great courage and calm; but after about five days the deadly tetanus began. Fisher Young was affected first. He was a boy of eighteen, and to the Bishop the dearest of the boys whom he had attached to the mission. Patteson was amazed by his staunch faith and patience, and his hold on God through the agonizing days that followed. 'Oh what love!' he said once, looking forward to Heaven, and all his words were full of hope and forgiveness. 'Poor Santa Cruz people', he said, and realizing how Patteson was suffering, 'Poor Bishop!' But he died at last, and they landed and buried him on an island that they knew. For a few more days it seemed as if the other two might both recover, but Edwin Nobbs died, though Pearce recovered. It was a terrible voyage of suspense and agony of mind and body. Fisher Young's death was an especial blow to Patteson.

He was my boy (he wrote to his sisters). I loved him as I think I never loved anyone else. I can hardly think of my room at Kohimarama without him. I try to be thankful. I think I am thankful really. . . . I never felt so utterly broken down as when I thought and think of the earthly side of it all, never perhaps so much realized the comfort and power of His Presence when I have had grace to dwell upon the heavenly and abiding side of it.

This grief and pain left its mark on him, and the voyages were less confident for a time.

He tells his sisters of the books that have comforted him. Jeremy Taylor's *Holy Dying*, the *Imitation*, but above all his Bible and Prayerbook. What Bible and Prayerbook people our nineteenth-century saints are!

In 1866 he was able, after negotiations with the Australian Government, to move his training school from Kohimarama to Norfolk Island where it remains to this day. It was warmer there, and a shorter voyage from the islands, and he felt that a life more akin to their own island life might be lived there. For he writes, again ahead of his time: 'I have for years thought that we seek in our missions a great deal too much to make English Christians of our converts. . . . We seek to denationalise these races whereas we ought really to change as little as possible only what is clearly incompatible with the simplest form of Christianity.'

About the same time he was writing to Joan:

When uncivilized races come into contact with civilized men they must either be condemned to a hopeless condition of inferiority, or they must be raised out of their state of ignorance and vice by appealing to those powers within them which God intended them to use, and the use of which will place them by God's blessing in the possession of whatever good things may be denoted by the words Religion and Civilization.

We make no distinction whatever between English and Melanesian members of the mission as such. No Melanesian is excluded from any office of trust. No classification is made of higher or lower kinds of work, of work befitting a black man, and work befitting a white man.

The move to Norfolk Island was completed in 1867. The Bishop then had with him five white men, two of them in orders, and sixty Melanesians, thirteen baptized and two confirmed. To the elder ones in this group he gave the greater part of his time.

As early as 1867 there was a report of the semi-legalized slave trading between the South Sea Islands, New Caledonia and Fiji. There was supposed to be a signed contract between the islanders and the traders, but Patteson wrote. 'We know the impossibility of making contracts with New Hebrides or Solomon Islands natives. It is a mere sham, the evasion of some law to procure colonial labour', but for the moment he felt that he could make no protest.

His first Christmas at Norfolk Island was happy. He ordained one priest and two deacons, and he felt that the next step would be the ordination to the deacon's office of a Melanesian, George Sarawia . . . 'my right hand with the Melanesians for years.'

But now he heard that he was to lose Bishop Selwyn who was going home to England to be Bishop of Lichfield:

> I shall often need you, and often sadly miss you (he wrote to Selwyn), but I do feel that it is right.
> I don't think I know yet what it is to me (he wrote to his sisters), but I don't feel at all sad or unhappy. I thank God for the blessing of thirteen years of his example and loving care of me.

He is thinking of those thirteen years in another letter home.

How are you thinking of me this anniversary? Thirteen years since I saw your faces. Oh how thankful I am that it is so long ago. It was very hard to bear for a long, long time. Last night as I lay in bed I thought of the words I said in church, the walk home—and then, black Monday. Well, I look back now and see that it was very hard at first, and I don't deny I found the mere bodily roughnesses very trying at first—but that has long, long passed. My present mode of life is altogether agreeable to me now.

I think of the islands and see them in my waking dreams, and it seems as if nothing was done, but I think again of what it was only a very short time ago, and, Oh, I do feel thankful, indeed amazed, and almost fearful.

He went to Auckland for the farewell service for Bishop Selwyn, and the Martins thought that he looked ill and tired and was feeling the cost of the parting very much. They all came back from the ship very much depressed, but Lady Martin describes how 'Dear Bishop Patteson roused himself from his natural depression, and set himself to cheer and comfort us all. How gentle and sympathizing he was . . . he went about from one to another in the kindest manner. I don't know how we should have got on without him.' It was cheering for him to ordain his first Melanesian deacon in 1868. George Sarawia was a man of very stirling character. 'He is not the cleverest of our scholars', wrote Patteson, 'but no one possesses the confidence of us all in the same degree.'

He went to Mota with George, to start him on his work there, and felt encouraged by the general improvement in the lives of the people there. 'There are not a few people here who are giving up their old habits, adopting new ways, accepting a stricter mode of life, forgoing advantages of one kind and another because they believe that this Good News, this Gospel is true.' But he deprecated tremendously giving them outward forms before they had discovered the inward meaning of Christian life. 'Anything is better than turning heathen into Pharisees.'

The 'Southern Cross' was in the wars again on this year's voyage, but that did not prevent them from going north and

making a call at the sad shores of Santa Cruz. The traders had
started a new device to lure men on board and kidnap them.
'The Bishop is ill, and can't come, and sends us to bring you to
him', they said to the islanders. Or, 'The Bishop is in Sydney, he
broke his leg getting into a boat and has sent us to bring you to
him.' It was all very puzzling. He was making preparations for a
voyage in 1870 when, at Norfolk Island, he suddenly fell
desperately ill of some internal inflammation. He thought he
was going to die, but nursed by Mr Nobbs he recovered enough
to go in April to Auckland to be properly doctored, and looked
after by Lady Martin, but the whole summer passed before he
was fit for work again, and he made no voyage among the
islands in 1870.

Day by day he sat by the fire too weak to move or to attend
to reading; yet when he could write letters again he said to the
sisters:

> The pain has been at times very severe, and yet I can't tell you of
> the very great happiness and actual enjoyment of many of those
> sleepless nights when perhaps at 2 a.m. I felt the pain subside, and
> prayer for rest if it were His Will was changed into thanksgiving
> for the relief; then as the fire flickered, came restful, peaceful,
> happy thoughts, mingled with much, I trust, heartfelt sorrow and
> remorse. And psalms seemed to have a new meaning, and prayers
> to be so real, and somehow there was a sense of a very near
> Presence.

He was told by the doctor that active exertion might bring
on his illness again so he writes home:

> I think it will come to my doing my work at Norfolk Island just
> as usual . . . but I think I may have to forgo some of the more
> risky and adventurous parts of the work on the Islands. I don't
> mean that I shall not take the voyages and stop about on the

Islands, but I must do it all more carefully and avoid much that of old I never thought about.

Lady Martin loved taking care of him. She wrote after his death:

He liked to have a quiet half-hour by the fire at night. Before I left him, I used to put his books near him, his Bible, his Hebrew psalter, and his father's copy of Bishop Andrews. He spoke once or twice with reverent holy awe and joy of sleepless nights when thoughts of God had filled his soul and sustained him. His face, always beautiful from the unworldly purity of its expression, was really as the face of an angel when he spoke of these things, and of the love and kindness he had received.

He kept hearing worrying news of the piratical labour traffic. He had a plan, which he put before the Governor, for certain vessels to be licensed to procure labour honestly, and all others treated like pirates and policed off the seas.

Meanwhile in his absence the 'Southern Cross' had made quite a good voyage with Mr Adkin and some of the others on board, and he himself made a short voyage before settling down for a time at Norfolk Island. It was an effort and he often felt ill, as on the day when he ordained Mr Bice as priest and wrote to Joan:

I was up as usual early this morning, and am not well and feeling queer, you see it is nearly three miles to the town, and the service will be nearly three hours, and I don't quite know how I shall get through it. . . . My chariot wheels often drag very heavily, I am not often in what you might call good spirits, and yet I am aware that I am writing now under the influence of a specially depressing disorder, and I may misinterpret my real state of mind.

It was the year of the Franco-German War, and he writes to his uncle: 'I can't write about politics. Then comes the fearful news of this fearful war. What am I to say to my Melanesians about it? Do these nations believe in the Gospel of Peace and goodwill? Is the Sermon on the Mount a reality or not? Oh this mighty belauded nineteenth-century civilization!'

So we come to his last journey. It began with a really cheering visit to Mota, which had somehow escaped visits from the raiders, and he was also feeling encouraged because he had managed to get into touch with the acting Consul at Fiji and hoped that through him he might be able to visit some of the raided islanders. George Sarawia had done good work at Mota; there were many baptisms of children, some of grown-up people, and regular classes; and all day people came to talk and to ask questions, bringing members of their family or friends. 'Scarce a moment's rest, but the work so interesting and so absorbing that I could scarcely feel weariness.' One man came up to him in the dark to speak to him, saying:

When a month ago I followed you, you said that if I wanted to know the meaning and power of this teaching I must pray. And I tried to pray, and it becomes easier as every day I go about in the morning and evening, and I don't know how to pray as I ought, but my heart is light and I know it is all true, and I have been wanting to tell you, and so have my friends, and we four talk together, and all want to be baptized.

And here is a snatch of his conversation with another who came, saying:

I do see the evil of my old life. I do believe in what you teach us, I feel in my heart new desires, new wishes, new hopes. The old life has become hateful to me, the new life is full of joy. . . . But it is so weighty, I am afraid. What if after making the promises I go back?

What do you doubt—God's power and love or your own weakness?

I don't doubt His power and love, but I am afraid.

64

Afraid of what?

Of falling away.

Doesn't He promise His help to those who need it?

Yes, I know that.

Do you pray?

I don't know how to pray properly, but I and my wife say: 'God, make our hearts light. Take away the darkness. We believe that You love us because You sent Jesus to become a man and die for us; but we can't understand it all. Make us fit to be baptized'.

Mota was the language that he had chosen for the translations from the Gospels and parts of the Prayerbook, which had been so absorbing to him, the product of his genius and his devotion. It would be possible for George's scholars to have these, and certain little books of instruction in their own tongue. Amongst all his other work he had kept his printers busy.

He left Mota hoping to return and to ordain George as his first priest in Melanesia. But the evil influence of the 'thief ships', as the islanders called them, was all-pervading in many of the islands. Some of the people had even asked Brooke: 'How was it that you and the Bishop came first and then the slaughterers? Did you send them?' Some longed for the Bishop to avenge them: 'Let Bisopé only bring a man of war, and get us vengeance.'

He went north from Mota and wrote to Selwyn:

Means of all sorts are employed, sinking canoes and capturing the natives, enticing men on board and getting them below and then securing the hatches and imprisoning them. It makes our work rather hazardous, except where we are thoroughly well known.

On Monday (D.V.) we go to Nukapu. I am aware that we shall be exposed to considerable risk, but I don't think there is very much cause for fear; first because at these small reef islands they know me pretty well; second, because last year I was on shore at Nukapu for some time. And now what will the next few days bring forth. It may be God's will that the opening for the Gospel may be given to us now. Sometimes I feel that I am almost too importunate in my longings for some beginnings here.

The 20th of September came and they set off for Nukapu, and Edward Wogale, one of his Melanesian boys, remembered: 'As we were going to that island where he died, he had spoken admirably and very strongly indeed about the death of Stephen, and then he went up ashore on that island, Nukapu.'

There was a little delay as the 'Southern Cross' made for the island, and he was afraid that the people in four canoes who were hovering about would be puzzled by it; so at 11.30 he desired that the boat should be lowered, and got into it with Joe Adkin, Stephen Taroniare, James Minapa and John Nonono. He called out to Brooke: 'Tell the Captain I may have to go ashore.' It was not possible to haul the ship's boat up on the reef, and the islanders proposed that the Bishop should come ashore in one of their canoes. He had always found that this seemed to allay suspicion, so he got into their canoe. The boat's crew of the 'Southern Cross' saw him land on the island. Suddenly the men in the boat were attacked by islanders in the canoes that had been waiting about. Three out of the four were struck before they could pull it out of range. They went back to the ship and landed the worst wounded; but Joe Adkin, himself hit, determined to go back for the Bishop and took three others with him. They had to wait till the tide was high enough to carry them across the reef, and they could see people on shore through a telescope; in the late afternoon it became possible to cross the reef and then two canoes came out towards them. One cast off from the other and went back to the shore. The other drifted towards them with something on board. They wondered at first if there were a man hidden under the matting who would spring up and attack them, but as they got nearer they knew who it was. It did not take long to see that it was a dead man who was covered by the matting. As they took him into the boat, they said to each other 'His body!' There lay the Bishop, the five wounds that caused his death had been given by club and arrow, only his face had not been touched, and there was a strange smile on it still. Across the breast they had laid a palm branch. Five knots in the leaves led the Melanesians to believe that his death was an act of vengenace for five men whom the traders had killed.

Joe Adkin wrote to his parents: 'Our Bishop is dead, killed by the natives at Nukapu yesterday. We got his body, and buried it in the sea yesterday. There was no sign of pain or fear on his face, just the look that he used to have when asleep—patient, and a little wearied.' Two of his friends followed the Bishop to death, poisoned by the arrows; Joe Adkin, who died in great agony, and Stephen, namesake of the first martyr. The other Melanesians who had been wounded recovered.

When Fisher and Edwin were martyred, Keble wrote to Patteson that the blood of the martyrs was the seed of the Church.

Patteson's own death was certainly seed of the Melanesian Church which grew and grows from strength to strength, but it also made a deep impact on English Christianity. It was beyond and above the struggles that were dividing church people at the time. It struck at the heart.

One of his Melanesian boys said: 'He did nothing to gain anything for himself alone, but he sought what he might keep others with, and then he worked with it, and the reason was his

pitifulness and his love. And again he did not despise anyone,
nor reject anyone with scorn, whether it were a white person or
a black person. He thought of them all as one, and he loved
them all alike.'

CHRISTINA ROSSETTI

1830—1894

THE lives of saints are so various. There are some flung overseas into the desperate struggle in a pagan country, there
are some whose lives are lived out in quite constricted circumstances. But we never get from them constricted powers or
vision. The door at the end of the narrow passage opens on to
Eternity.

A poet was paying a visit to an obscure house in Bloomsbury
to make an enquiry about the whereabouts of a friend, and there
he found two of the family of the friend whom he was seeking
—an old man, sitting by the fire, and a young girl standing
writing at a desk by the window. She was a 'slight girl', he
noted, 'with a serious regular profile, dark against the wintry
light without.' She intrigued him as he stood talking to the
father of his friend, all the more for the fact that 'she had turned
at my entrance, made a most formal and graceful curtsey, and
then resumed her writing'. She was seventeen, this slight girl
Christina, who was writing and obliterating herself so success-
fully, the youngest of a devoted family circle, who were
delightfully easy in their relationship with one another.

She was at home with her father, Gabriele Rossetti, and not
out teaching like her mother and elder sister, probably because
she had been for a year or two the delicate one. They were poor

this Rossetti family, but never sordidly poor. The father had come to England at the height of the Risorgimento period, when there were rich patrons to assist an Italian suffering for his rebel affinities, but by now the ebb had come, the patrons were dead, and it was necessary for the family to earn what they could by their various gifts. Maria the elder sister and the mother had teaching work and the father gave Italian lessons until his eyes began to fail. Gabriel the poet and painter was not earning much, William Michael, who seems to have been the solid one of the family, had a small post at the Inland Revenue Office. And then there was Christina. She was lovely to look at. The picture that Gabriel made of her when she was sixteen, with the high brow, the regular gentle features, the firm well-shaped chin, and the great serious eyes, and the dark hair, in its ringlets then, must have delighted the artist brother, who used her often as a model. She began writing when she was quite young, and her mother's father, Grandfather Polidori, had a little volume of her early verse privately printed when she was seventeen. It was perhaps cruel kindness, for she was to find out like so many young poets how difficult it is for the unknown poet to get work received. She minded as all sensitive writers do:

> Sometimes I said it is an empty name
> I long for, to a name why should I give
> The peace of all the days I have to live?
> Yet gave it all the same.

Her poetry welled up in her, and she poured it out. Though she revised it, for she loved finished work, she did not plan it. 'Christina's habits of writing were eminently of the spontaneous kind', wrote the brother who loved her best. The little washstand in her tiny bedroom was her poet's desk, she vanished there to put down a flying thought.

All the Rossetti children had been born in England, but all had spoken much Italian with their father, and Christina wrote happily in both languages; and some of the grace of her writing seems to come from that other tongue, some of the confident rhythm and rhyme from her heritage in a language where rhyme is no elusive hope but a natural certainty. Her taste in her teens was for sacrificial things, martyrdoms, forsaken lovers, nuns fretting 'at their convent's narrow walls'. Her own poor health with its frustrations may have turned her towards these wistful longing lyrics, but maybe it was also an early breath of that *nostalgie de l'infinie* which was so characteristic of her later work. The most considerable of these early poems, is a visionary one called *The Dead City*. Some of that gift that she had later for heaping up sumptuous lists of words is here:

> And the apricot and pear
> And the pulpy fig were there,
> Cherries and dark mulberries,
> Bunchy currants, strawberries
> And the lemon wan and fair.

At the end of her rather frightening vision of the Dead City a sense of her poet's vocation touches her:

> Yes once more I stood alone
> Where the happy sunlight shone,
>   And a gentle wind was sighing,
>   And the little birds were flying,
> And the dreariness was gone.
>
> All these things that I have said
> Awed me, and made me afraid.
>   What was I that I should see
>   So much hidden mystery?
> And I straightway knelt and prayed.

The most lovely of these early poems is especially hers. How skilled she was in the short line, with its need for simplicity! How she filled it with her own singing tone!

Gone were but the Winter,
  Come were but the Spring,
I would go to a covert
  Where the birds sing;

Where in the white thorn
  Singeth a thrush,
And a robin sings
  In the holly bush.

Full of fresh scents
  Are the budding boughs
Arching high over
  A cool green house;

Full of sweet scents
  And whispering air
Which sayeth softly:
  'We spread no snare;

'Here dwell in safety,
  Here dwell alone,
With a clear stream
  And a mossy stone.

'Here the sun shineth
  Most shadily;
Here is heard an echo
  Of the far sea,
Though far off it be.'

That was written in the spring of her seventeenth year.

In some ways she had the good fortune to obtain a rare training in verse writing, for the Rossetti family played that delightful Victorian game of 'Bouts rimés', and how well they played it, turning out sonnets in ten minutes, criticising each other's verses seriously and frankly! These were the five-finger-exercises of poetry, and really gave Christina a technique which was enduring. To be the youngest of a family straining a little perhaps to keep up with Gabriel, and William Michael, who only forsook poetry to keep the family in daily bread, was a considerable apprenticeship.

And then there was the Pre-Raphaelite Brotherhood. Her elder brother Gabriel was a focus for men's dreams, those dreams which emerged in such a brotherhood as has never been seen since. It flowed from the same spring as the Tractarian Movement, that revolt against the mediocre and complacent, that harking back to something more pure, more primitive, to a forgotten yet eternal beauty. The Rossettis had grown up among rebels, and now to the young Christina, these men who were her brothers' friends, with their hunger and thirst after a loveliness that they were both discovering and creating, were most stimulating company. She counted in their gatherings, for though she was generally silent, she could sometimes make a clear and apt comment which mattered to the others. She had a voice of peculiar sweetness with a certain precision, perhaps arising from her background of Italian speech. The young men called her the Queen of the Pre-Raphaelites.

Certainly the least distinguished of the group fell in love with her, in her late teens, and she with him. Was it perhaps her humility or her charity that attached her to James Collinson? 'She was markedly his superior', wrote her partial brother, William Michael. She had often seen him before Gabriel ad-

73

mitted him to a rather reluctant P.R.B. They found him tame
and sleepy. Christina had watched him in Church, at Christ
Church, Albany St, where she and her mother and Maria went
on Holy days and Sundays, and then suddenly he was there no
more, and she found that he had joined the Roman Church. It
was this that made her refuse his first offer, though she loved him.
Here we must begin to consider the depth of Christina's loyalty
to the Anglican Communion, and especially to the Tractarian
movement. In a very enduring way it was part of her growth,
for she was really a member of it in the exact sense of the word.
James Collinson was of different stuff, and he proceeded to
return to Anglicanism, and was accepted by Christina. But
neither he nor his family to whom she paid an unsatisfying visit
were really her stuff. It is almost a relief when he veers again
towards Rome, and Christina lets him go. But this early turning
aside from earthly love for the sake of something more precious,
though it left an aching emptiness in her life was a sort of introduction to the frustration and suffering, the relinquishment
which was so much a part of her spiritual life.

She met him once or perhaps only passed him, and fainted
away in the street, and the trouble affected her health. She got
some news of Collinson from her brothers, and remembered to
ask about his very indifferent pictures. But there was pain in it all.

> O unforgotten!
> An unforgotten load of love,
> A load of grief all griefs above,
> A blank, blank nest, without its dove.

The ten years between 1850 and 1860 were a time of strange
frustration for Christina. She was sometimes seriously ill, the
prospect of her writing bringing her fame and recognition as a
poet seemed to evaporate with the breakup of the P.R.B., and

the downfall of the *Germ*. The family were very poor, and she could not meet the poverty in any way that brought real relief, though she tried translating and teaching. Then there were breaks in the family that had seemed so solid. Mrs Rossetti's father who had loved Christina's poetry died, and so did the grandmother Polidori. Then when it seemed that William Michael's generosity was going to free them from an ungrateful period of school teaching at Frome, the father died. And Dante married a girl whom they never quite accepted, though Christina saw how lovely she was, and the marriage ended in tragedy.

Perhaps more puzzling to Christina, after her rather propitious start in the *Germ*, and the *Athenaeum*, was the fact that she could find no publisher for her poetry. And she minded because she knew that her work was good:

> I am not unaware (she wrote to Professor Aytoun) that the editor of a magazine looks with dread and contempt upon the offering of a nameless rhymester, and that the feeling is in nineteen cases out of twenty a just and salutary one. It certainly is not for me to affirm that I am the one twentieth in question, but speaking as I am to a poet, I hope I shall not be misunderstood as guilty of egotism or foolish vanity when I say that my love for what is good in the works of others teaches me that there is something above the despicable in mine; that poetry is with me, not a mechanism but an impulse and a reality, and that I know my aims in writing to be pure and directed to that which is true and right.

In the end it was Gabriel who helped her to get her first book published. *Uphill* had achieved a place in Macmillan's Magazine and was hailed as the masterpiece that it is, one of Christina's spare poems written with an amazing economy. And Gabriel was encouraged to talk to Macmillan and to tell him about other of Christina's poems lying hidden in little exercise books in her lovely handwriting, and eventually it is Macmillan who produces her first book of poems in 1861: *Goblin Market, and other poems*, with a frontispiece full of wombatty goblins by Dante Gabriel, and containing such other lovelinesses as *When I am dead* and *An Apple Gathering* and *Sound Sleep*.

At the end of this volume Christina had made a special section which she called *Devotional Pieces*. Did she think it more reverent to separate these from the Goblins, or did she want her poems to be judged on two levels or in two different ways? It is worth while as we are considering her spirtual history to look at these sixteen poems carefully. They do reflect a good deal of the stress and weariness and frustration of the ten previous years; on the whole they are sad poems, poems of an oppressed soul with wings outstretched but somehow unable to fly. They are poems of one who is waiting, as a tree waits for spring, with buds on the bare boughs, a soul in the pains of relinquishment. Something she has already relinquished; sometimes bitterly she calls it the world, sometimes it is youth and beauty, sometimes opportunity. The spirit of the whole section might be found in her poem *Passing Away*, one of the poems which she called *Old and New Year Ditties*, a most beautiful poem in itself. Swinburne hailed it as 'so much the noblest of Sacred poetry in English that none is second'.

> Passing away, saith the World, passing away:
> Chances, beauty, and youth sapped day by day:
> Thy life never continueth in one stay.
> Is the eye waxen dim, is the dark hair changing to grey
> That has won neither laurel nor bay?
> I shall clothe myself in spring and bud in May:
> Thou, rootstricken, shall not rebuild thy decay
>   On my bosom for aye.
> Then I answered: Yea.

Passing away, saith my soul, passing away:
With its burden of fear and hope, and labour and play,
Hearken what the past doth witness and say:
Rust in thy gold, a moth in thine array,
A canker is in thy bud, thy leaf must decay.
At midnight, at cockrow, at morning one certain day
Lo, the bridegroom shall come and shall not delay;
Watch thou and pray.
Then I answered: Yea.

Passing away, saith my God, passing away:
Winter passeth after the long delay:
New grapes on the vine, new figs on the tender spray,
Turtle calleth to turtle in Heaven's May.
Though I tarry, wait for Me trust Me, watch and pray:
Arise, come away, night is past, and lo it is day
My love, My sister, My spouse, thou shalt hear me say.
Then I answered: Yea.

And again in her poem *Amen* with which she ends this section,
is the same sense of an end and a beginning.

It is over. What is over?
    Nay, now much is over truly!
Harvest days we toiled to sow for;
    Now the sheaves are gathered newly,
Now the wheat is garnered duly.

It is finished. What is finished?
    Much is finished known or unknown:
Lives are finished; time diminished;
    Was the fallow field left unsown?
    Will these buds be always unblown?

It suffices. What suffices?
    All suffices reckoned rightly:
Spring shall bloom where now the ice is,

Roses make the bramble sightly,
And the quickening sun shine brightly,
And the latter wind blow lightly,
And my garden teem with spices.

There has come a new definite period in her life, an entering into a new relationship with God, and acceptance of a new kind of life. *Goblin Market* is her old self, but she will never write anything quite like it again; though that tumbling luscious hurry of the Goblins musn't disguise from us that *Goblin Market* is also in her old strain, a poem of sacrifice, a turning of the dangerous fruits into the saving fruits by the devotion of one sister to the other. 'Much is over', she says in *Amen*, and much was over, and yet much was to come—the hardest sacrifices, the longest patience, but never again, I think, that despairing frustration.

Everyday life took on a different shape. The father was dead, and Gabriel's wife was dead. The home party were now Mrs Rossetti, and her two sisters, the Polidori aunts, who became later Christina's special charge, and William Michael, coming and going a good deal between his mother's home, and Gabriel's rather strange Chelsea establishment with the menagerie in the back garden.

Christina was getting a good deal of understanding appreciation of her first book of poems. But for her the main thing in the 60's was a friendship that was going to be as costly as it was precious.

When old Gabriele Rossetti was on his deathbed, an ex-pupil came to visit him. This was Charles Bagot Cayley, a scholar, a very clever linguist, a man lovable in his vagueness and sweetness of nature. His visit gave great pleasure to the Rossetti family, and he saw something of them from then on, but his special friendship with Christina did not begin until she saw him quite often with

Dante Gabriel in 1862. It was the time of Lizzie Rossetti's death, and Gabriel was much with his family and the quiet scholar became something more than a friend to Christina. She accuses herself of having treated him badly, and at any rate he felt that he might propose to her in 1864, so that she must have encouraged the shy man in his hopes. She certainly loved him with all the tenderness of her nature, and gave him all sorts of intimate pet names, he was her buzzard, her blindest mole, her wombat, a little animal to which Gabriel and Christina were very much attached. There was deep love between them. But then there was also truth, and truth separated them. To Christina truth was the Church, its teaching, its claims, its glory. To Cayley truth was something less committed. He was in fact an agnostic, not I think an irreligious man, but a questioner of that which was to Christina essential. So she put this love away also, or rather she put marriage away; she would not marry him. William Michael wondered if it was a question of means, and offered most generously to help them, but Christina, as she thanked him, wrote:

> As to money, I might be selfish enough to wish that were the only bar, but you see from my point of view it is not.
>
> The love of Christ (she wrote long after) like a touchstone has tested much human affection, and over and over again has proved it dross. Yet now and then two who have differed—and two who differ cannot both hold the entire truth—have loved on faithfully, believing and hoping the best of each other, one (perhaps each) praying for the other, both alike exercising themselves to have always a conscience void of offence. In such a case, where both have loved the truth and have accounted it 'Great . . . and mighty above all things' there surely remains a strong consolation of hope to flee unto. For can an utter alien from God love Truth and make sacrifices for Truth's sake?

This time the man who wanted her was worthy of her; and she loved him all his life long—and he returned her love.

But the cost of this renunciation was fabulous. Some of it she hid away in a series of little poems in Italian, which William found locked in her desk after she died, some under a disguise she revealed in a sonnet sequence *Monna Innominata* which she wrote in the character of a mediaeval woman.

> Many in after times will say of you
> 'He loved her,' while of me what will they say?
> Not that I loved you more than just in play,
> For fashion's sake as idle women do.
> Even let them prate; who know not what we knew
> Of love and parting in exceeding pain,
> Of parting hopeless here to meet again,
> Hopeless on earth, and heaven is out of view.
> But by my heart of love laid bare to you,
> My love that you can make not void or vain,
> Love that forgoes you, but to claim anew
> Beyond this passage of the gate of death,
> I charge you at the judgement make it plain
> My love of you was life, and not a breath.

And a rough translation of one of her Italian poems runs:

> What shall I give to Thee Jesus Lord of Love?
> That which I love most, that I give to Thee:
> Accept it from me, Lord Jesus my God,
> Accept my one dear love—my very heart.

'Years passed', wrote her brother, 'she became an elderly and an old woman, and she loved the scholarly recluse to the last day of his life, and to the last day of her own, his memory.'

He wrote to her, sometimes, rather stilted unrevealing letters respecting perhaps her position, and they saw each other from time to time; indeed a week before Cayley's death, William

Michael found him taking a hand at whist with Christina, her mother, and one of the Polidori aunts. His sister wrote to Christina after his death: 'You were I *know*, the friend he valued most.' He left her all his manuscript translations though she had only suggested 'Some trifle that you had been fond of and perhaps had used would be precious to me.'

'She put love from her with both hands, and yearned for it unceasingly', wrote Ford Maddox Hueffer. He forgot perhaps that she still had two strains of love, even three, which even her ascetic scrupulous sense would admit; the family love especially for her mother and William Michael, the holy love for Christ, and the love for her art, her words—for all poets do love their words, their rhythms, and their conceptions. Undoubtedly Christina's poetry was deepened and enriched by her sacrificed love for Cayley.

'The life of this marvellous woman, who stands alone in the forefront of the world's female poets, was clouded and frustrated by her sorrows, and her repudiations. She knew how exquisite life was before she pushed away from her lips the cup of its enchantments, and it is this which gives to her finest songs and sonnets their penetrating charm of valour and music', wrote Edmund Gosse.

Let us look at her as Cayley saw her, before illness had altered the beauty that the Pre-Raphaelites had loved, and which Dante Gabriel drew in 1866. The eyes which were so beautiful and so shining that Holman Hunt used them for a model for the eyes of Christ in the *Light of the World* are still her most striking feature. The calm even lines of her face, the strong jaw line, the well-shaped nose, the full but quiet mouth, the smooth hair which never lost its gloss or colour give an impression of attained serenity; a face so William Michael wrote, 'very chaste in outline, and distinguished in expression.' 'Her hands were delicate', he adds, 'and her figure might be called good without being remarkably fine.' Such a Christina her 'Blindest Buzzard' saw, or perhaps did not see.

And when she spoke: 'Her utterance was clear', wrote her brother, 'her delivery, as indeed her whole aspect marked unmistakably by sincerity and consideration for others.'

Here is the impression made upon a child, Grace Gilchrist, who saw her about this time. 'She was then a dark-eyed slender lady, in the plenitude of her poetic powers. To my child's eyes she appeared like some fairy princess who had come from the sunny South to play with me. In appearance she was Italian with olive complexion and deep hazel eyes. She possessed too the beautiful Italian voice all the Rossettis were gifted with, a voice made up of strange, sweet inflections, which rippled into silvery modulations in sustained conversations, making ordinary English words fall upon the ear with soft foreign intonation, though she pronounced the words themselves with the purest of English accents.'

Her voice seems always to have struck people. Watts Dunton writing of his first meeting at D.G.'s studio says: 'I heard a voice precise, formal, yet sweet as a silver bell say, 'Yes Gabriel, they are the loveliest apple blossoms I have ever seen in a picture.' There was something in the tone of the voice that banished all my awe of the saint and I entered the room. Later, after a little talk he adds that he thought her ' a very saint, no doubt, but a playful one.'

Another picture of her is on her visit to Penhill Castle in Argyllshire, where she went to stay with Miss Boyd, a friend of the Bell Scotts. At Penhill the room assigned to the shy, dark-haired lady from London looked out upon an old garden, and had a little four-cornered window at which the lady used to stand for hours together, her elbows on the sill, her hands supporting her face—lost in meditation.

And now what is it that she is to give us with that generosity of the Saints?

I think one of her special gifts is her delight, her trust, her rejoicing in the 'Life of the World to come.' She is so often there with the Saints and the Martyrs, and the Angels, adoring the Lord to whom she has turned herself. Like the negro hymn writer her theme is so often 'Heaven, heaven, heaven.' All the colour and richness, and glory of her poetical inheritance she gave, obeying literally the Lord's word: 'Lay up for yourselves treasures in Heaven':

> Jerusalem makes melody
>   For simple joy of heart;
> An organ of full compass she
>   One tuned through every part:
> While not to day or night belong
> Her matins and her evensong,
>   The one thanksgiving of her throng.
>
> Jerusalem a garden is,
>   A garden of delight;
> Leaf, flower, and fruit make fair her trees,
>   Which see not day or night
> Beside her River clear and calm
> The Tree of Life grows with the Palm,
> For triumph, and for food and balm.
>
> Jerusalem, where song nor gem
>   Nor fruit nor waters cease,
> God bring us to Jerusalem,
>   God bring us home in peace;

The strong who stand, the weak who fall,
The first and last, the great and small,
Home one by one, home one and all.

To her it was essentially home.

Home by different ways. Yet all
    Homeward bound through prayer and praise,
Young with old, and great with small,
    Home by different ways.

Many nights and many days
    Wind must bluster, rain must fall,
Quake the quicksand, shift the haze.

Life has called and death will call
    Saints who praying kneel at gaze,
Ford the flood or leap the wall,
    Home by different ways.

(Notice the Roundel form of this poem, for Christina loved
this form with its repetitions, and its two rhymes. She uses it so
often in her songs of Heaven and the Lord. Notice also how the
one qualifying adjective *different* gains by the fact that there are
no other qualifying adjectives in the poem.)

And to this Home the saints are flocking, and she loves to be
of their company. Her poem *All Saints*, is a sort of sanctified
Goblin Market, with its short line, and tremendous sense of
movement.

They are flocking from the East
And the West,
They are flocking from the North
And the South,
Every moment setting forth
From realm of snake or lion,

Swamp or sand,
Ice or burning.
Greatest and least,
Palm in hand
And praise in mouth,
They are flocking up the path
To their rest,
Up the path that hath
No returning.
Up the steeps of Zion
They are mounting,
Coming, coming,
Throngs beyond man's counting.

.   .   .   .

And she sees them, as we have learnt to love them in her
Martyrs' Song.

Strong as the lion, pure as the dove,
With open arms and hearts of love.

Yes, the Communion of Saints was very dear to her, and
when later she was too ill to write much poetry, she made a
book, a prose book, about the Black-letter saints, giving each
flower, a rather hidden flower, and a gem, and a prayer, and
sometimes a poem, a special offering which she named: *Called
to be Saints*.

It is so difficult to choose from among the many poems which
show this 'lover of the Lord' revealing herself for our gain.
William Michael probably published more than she would ever
have published herself, but his book of her collected poems does
give his beloved Christina in all her many-sided genius. We
see her telling a village story in such moving and clear verse,

singing heavenly little rhymes to a beloved baby, watching the seasons with sweet melancholy, sorrowing and hoping for love, and then this talking, sighing to the Lord, with unswerving but deeply tested trust and love. Some of these Divine love songs must be put into any account of her, but whichever I choose, her lovers will wonder why I did not choose another.

Here is quite an early poem when she is in her twenties, showing her as the mystic even at that early date:

> My Lord, my Love! in pleasant pain
>   How often have I said,
> 'Blessed that John who on Thy breast
>   Laid down his head'.
> It was that contact all divine
>   Transformed him from above,
> And made him amongst men the man
>   To show forth Holy Love
>
> Yet shall I envy blessed John?
>   Nay not so verily,
> Now that Thou, Lord, both Man and God,
>   Dost dwell in me:
> Up building with Thy Manhood's might
>   My frail humanity:
> Yes Thy Divinehood pouring forth,
>   In fulness filling me
>
> Me, Lord, Thy temple consecrate,
>   Even me to Thee alone;
> Lord reign upon my willing heart
>   Which is Thy throne:
> To Thee the Seraphim fall down
>   Adoring round Thy house;
> For which of them hath tasted Thee,
>   My Manna and my Spouse?

Now that Thy life lives in my soul
   And sways and warms it through,
I scarce seem lesser than the world,
   Thy temple too
O God, who dwellest in my heart
   My God who fillest me
The broad immensity itself
   Hath not encompassed Thee.

Here is one held in her deep simplicity.

Leaf from leaf Christ knows;
Himself the Lily and the Rose:

Sheep from sheep Christ tells;
Himself the Shepherd, no one else:

Star and star He names,
Himself outblazing all their flames:

Dove by dove He calls
To set each on the golden walls:

Drop by drop, He counts
The flood of ocean as it mounts:

Grain by grain, His hand
Numbers the innumerable sand.

Lord, I lift to Thee
In peace what is and what shall be:

Lord, in peace I trust
To Thee all spirits and all dust.

It is a sure, but quite humble love.

> Give me the lowest place; not that I dare
> Ask for that lowest place, but Thou hast died
> That I might live and share
> Thy glory by Thy side.
>
> Give me the lowest place: or if for me
> That lowest place too high, make one more low
> Where I may sit and see
> My God and love Thee so.

And here again, in the utmost simplicity, she commends herself to her Lord.

> Lord Jesus, who would think that I am Thine?
>   Ah who would think,
> Who sees me ready to turn back or sink,
>   That Thou art mine?
>
> I cannot hold Thee fast tho' Thou art mine:
>   Hold Thou me fast,
> So earth shall know at last, and heaven at last
>   That I am Thine.

And this is her often repeated claim:

> Love is the key of life and death,
>   Of hidden heavenly mystery:
> Of all Christ is, of all He saith,
>   Love is the key.
>
> As three times to His saint He saith,
>   He saith to me, He saith to thee,
> Breathing His grace conferring Breath:
>   'Lovest thou Me'?

Ah, Lord, I have such feeble faith,
    Such feeble hope to comfort me:
But love it is, is strong as death,
    And I love Thee.

It is difficult to stop quoting, but there are some other things
which one wants to know about a saint. How was she nourished?
What was it like to be with her? First of all, as with Mother
Cecile later, she was a tremendous reader of the Bible, reading
it as a poet reads, with a heart open to its symbolism, using it,
as we shall see when we look at her prose works, very simply.
The controversies of her time were not very important to her.
'There were few things she more disliked than "Evidences of
Christianity",' wrote William Michael. As a mystic her evidence
was an inward authority. 'Her attitude of mind', her brother
continues, 'was "I believe because I am told to believe, and I
know that the authority which tells me to believe is the only
real authority extant, God." ' Her faith was shaped according
to the Tractarian form. She was a most true, and unquestioning
follower of that way of conceiving of Christianity. First of all
Canon Burrows, who was Vicar of Christ Church, Albany
Street, the Church of her youthful days, and afterwards Dr
Littledale, who became her director, were the priests who
served her spirit. For the last named she had a special admiration,
his courage, and humour through periods of ill-health and pain
inspired her, who had so much pain to bear.

Anglo-Catholicism gave her the saints, and the colour and
beauty gave her the holy seasons which she loved and celebrated
in many poems and prayers, gave her a sacramental outlook on
life which was very near to her own genius, for she loved to
discover God in his works, to penetrate into eternity through
small beasts and flowers.

If she had lived fifty years later she would have found many companions among the mystics. But at her date no one was taking much notice of the mystics or writing about them. She had no means of knowing Lady Julian, Richard Rolle, Walter Hilton, or the author of the *Cloud of Unknowing*. She read and loved that master guide-book of the saints, the *Imitation of Christ*, and she also knew and used St Augustine's *Confessions*, and the more homely *Pilgrim's Progress*. She was familiar with Plato, in translation for she had no Greek, and all the Italian in her fed upon Dante. She might have found George Herbert, for he was read by pious people at her date, but she never mentions him.

After her dismissal of Cayley, I think she turned to Christ with a new committed love. Here she could spend herself, and give in the way she craved to do.

> To give, to give, not to receive!
>   I long to pour myself, my soul,
> Not to keep back or count or leave,
>   But king with king to give the whole.
>
> I long for one to stir my deep—
>   I have had enough of help and gift,
> I long for one to search and sift,
>   Myself, to take myself and keep.

The family claimed much of her love, especially her mother. The love of those two is one of the lovely mother and daughter relationships, unpossessive and clear of any claimfulness. The brothers and sisters were enclosed in the family love, for William Michael she had a steadfast affection, and wrote to him in their old age to say, 'so long as I have you, I have one very dear person left.' He perhaps guessed much of her suffering, and took her and her mother to Italy in 1865. They drove over the

St Gothard, and Christina remembered long afterwards, a mass of tiny blue forget-me-nots at the summit (unforgotten, and never to be forgotten, she wrote). Another memorable evening she and William Michael spent rowing about on Lake Como.

> All things then waxed musical; each star
> Sang on its course, each breeze sang on its car,
> All harmonies sang to senses wide awake
> All things in tune, my self not out of tune,
> Those nightingales were nightingales indeed.

They went on to Milan, Pavia, Verona, sightseeing vigorously; it was with a strange homesickness that she turned north again.

> To come back from the sweet South to the North,
>   Where I was born, bred, look to die;
> Come back to do my days work in its day,
>   Play out my play:
>   Amen, Amen say I.

> .   .   .   .

> But when our swallows fly back to the South,
> To the sweet South, to the sweet South,
> The tears may come into my eyes
> On the old wise,
> And the sweet name to my mouth.

She wrote to a friend: 'Such imaginable beauties and grandeurs of nature as we beheld, no pen could put on paper, so I obviously need not exert myself to tell you what Lucerne was like, or what the lovely majesty of St Gothard, or what the Lake of Como with its nightingale accompaniment or what as much of Italy as we saw to our half-Italian hearts.'

Her second book of poems: *The Prince's Progress* was published soon after this vist to Italy. *Goblin Market* had gone into two editions which pleased Christina, though we are glad that she was human enough to be a little jealous of Jean Inglow's eight editions, much as she admired the writer. Dante Gabriel had concerned himself with the new book, his suggestions fortunately were not followed out by Christina who laughed at them, and took her own way while pleased by his care for her work. Gabriel had wished for a tournament to be inserted into *The Prince's Progress* but Christina holds up hands of horror. 'How shall I express my feelings about the terrible tournament?'

In the devotional section of this new book perhaps the best poem is the well-known *Martyrs Song*, parts of which we sing in our hymn, *What are these that glow from afar*.

> God the Father give us grace
> To walk in the light of Jesu's Face:
> God the Son give us a part
> In the hiding place of Jesu's Heart:
> God the Spirit so hold us up
> That we may drink of Jesu's cup:
> God Almighty, God Three in One,
> God Almighty, God alone.

So we sing, but the lines have been transposed a little, still Christina would probably not have minded since her last two lines of climax at the end of the poem have been kept in their right place.

1871 brought her terribly disabling illness, Grave's Disease, which altered her lovely appearance, took away physical strength, made her incapable of sustained writing for the time, and left her with permanent heart trouble. She was immensely brave through it all. 'She shows a really remarkable constancy,' wrote William Michael, 'and the worst shafts of fate find her their equal.' She must write something and there was a baby belonging to Arthur Cayley, brother of her Charles for whom she began to write *Sing Song*, one of the most delicate set of little rhymes, real songs of innocence with a Blakean flavour. I think she sometimes left off thinking about the baby, though the sweet child-likeness continues, and her own transparent style.

> What are heavy? Sea sand and sorrow:
> What are brief? Today and tomorrow:
> What are frail? Spring blossoms and youth:
> What are deep? The Ocean and truth.

That is not for a child. But there are countless little poems full of furry animals, and lambs, and singing birds, and delicate flowers, as well as some very practical ones connected with the multiplication table. We almost love her best, childless Christina, in this sweet elusive strain that springs up to transfigure her time of weakness, in this gaiety that discounts her disfigurement and weariness. We remember how her cousins used to wonder at the child Christina who picked up little creatures with such a strange confidence.

The disease wore off and its most depressing symptoms receded, but Christina bore the marks of it till her death. She began to write more regularly again, not poetry to any extent. Four prose works, and one book of prayers give us a good deal of insight into her quietly disciplined mind and spirit where the rainbow is so intimately one with the cloud. 'The heavenliest kind of Christian', she had once written, 'exhibits more bow than cloud, walking the world in a continual thanksgiving.'

These prose books which she made at the request of S.P.C.K. were in a way duty books, books which she thought that she ought to write. The Bible and the Saints are their inspiration, and one of them, *Time Flies*, gives us an intimate picture of her reverent obedient aspiring spirit to which she applies the spur of the saint, and the rein of the governed life, among her thoughts she tucks in here a poem—some of the most exquisite are here— and sometimes a reminiscence of her childhood, or some quietly observed moment in daily life such as this one:

One day long ago I sat in a certain garden by a certain ornamental water. I sat so long and so quietly that a wild garden creature or two made its appearance: a water rat perhaps, or a water haunting bird. Few have been my personal experiences of the sort and this one gratified me. I was absorbed that afternoon in anxious thought yet the slight incident pleased me. If by any chance people noticed me they may have thought how dull and blank I must be feeling: and partly they would be right but partly wrong. Many I hope whom we pity as even wretched, may in reality as I was at that moment, be conscious of some small secret fount of pleasure: a bubble perhaps, yet lit by a dancing rainbow. I hope so and I think so: for we and all creatures are in God's hand, and God loves us.

Here is another entry:

Our room, as God builds and makes it for us, is likewise our nest, and a nest is surely the very homeliest idea of a home. A nest implies, suggests, so much. A circumference in comfortable proportion to its inhabitant's size. Warmth and softness: For so 'He giveth His beloved sleep'. Pure air, bright sunshine; leafy shade sufficient to satisfy a very Jonah. A windy branch whereon to rock safely. Wind and rain heard yet little felt. A storm indeed sometimes but as the exception not as the rule. Most of all by way of comfort a nest suggests an overhanging presence of love. A brooding breast sheltering its cherished nestlings. A love ready to face death in their defence.

When room and way are too great for us let us think of Him who prepared our present 'nest' and carries His little ones, and who desires to see in each of us of the travail of His soul and to be satisfied. And who eighteen hundred years ago comforted His disciples, saying 'In my Father's House are many mansions; if it were not so I would have told you—I go to prepare a place for you'.

The other prose work which I find especially characteristic of her own religion is *Called to the Saints*. Here she has revelled in finding symbols, and special flowers, and gems from the Heavenly Jerusalem for each of her nineteen Blackletter saints, and she has given each a prayer, of which I find this one of St Simon and St Jude full of her own approach, very humble and in a way fearful, yet full of glory.

O God one Fountain of glory, whose glory invests apostles, missionaries, martyrs, and Whose Holy Spirit within them is a Spirit of glory and grace, we praise Thee for Thy blessed Saints Simon and Jude, now hidden in the glory of Thy Presence, and awaiting the glory that shall be revealed when the Son of Man cometh in His glory: Wherefore we ourselves being feeble persons crippled by shortcomings, blotted by sins, beset by infirmities, misusing prolonged life, overhung by death, fearful of that which loometh beyond death, do most earnestly implore Thee to make our cause Thy cause and our quarrel Thy quarrel: sparing us and reviving our strength before we go hence and are no more seen, washing us whiter than snow renewing us unto righteousness, holding up our goings in Thy paths that our footsteps slip not, granting us a good courage, giving us no more fear than is needful and holy, no more than may serve to guard love and than shall be cast out by perfect love.
Amen, O God, for the brightness of Thy glory's sake, our Saviour Jesus Christ the King of Glory. Amen.

There is Christina, her fears, as Greatheart said of Mr Fearing, are about her 'acceptance at the last', perhaps because she saw the Glory so much more clearly than most of us, and could not believe that it was for her.

One of the things that she wrote at this time was a book of

prayers *Annus Domini*—one for each day of the year. They are
all addressed to our Lord. Here is one of them:

> O Lord Jesus Christ, whose banner over us is love: bring all men,
> I entreat Thee, under obedience to Thy Banner, and lead us
> whithersoever Thou wilt. Amen.

The other three books are not so important, they show mostly
her utter love of the Bible and her detailed study of it. *Letter and
Spirit* has some strangely wise and pointed teaching about
everyday failings.

The Rossetti family had an awkward family question to
settle in 1876. William Michael had married Lucy Madox
Browne in 1874, and at first the family tried the nearly impossible plan of the joint household. They had known Lucy for
some years, and the marriage was acceptable to all of them.
Christina had written to her on her engagement, 'I should like
to be a dozen years younger, and worthier every way of becoming your sister; but, such as I am be sure of my loving welcome
to you as my dear sister and friend'. Just as a sidelight on Christina's humility, it is worthwhile to quote the letter she wrote to
Lucy when she and her mother changed house and joined up
with the Polidori aunts. 'I hope that when two roofs shelter us
and when faults which I regret are no longer your daily trial, that
we may regain some of the liking which we had as friends, and
which I should wish to be only the more tender and warm now
that we are sisters. Don't please despair of my doing better.'

So Christina and Mrs Rossetti went to 30 Torrington Square,
which was their home till death. Maria was dying now in her
sisterhood, and it was a rather heavy burden that Christina took
on in the care of the three older ladies; perhaps it aged her too.
It was in this house that she wrote her prose works, moving
from room to room to suit the infirmities of the old ladies; she

finally made the drawing room her work room. People who went to visit her there, found the atmosphere full of a deep peace. When Alice Meynelle heard that Katharine Tynan Higson was to go to see Christina Rossetti she said to her: 'You are going to have the privilege of seeing a Saint'—it was like that to go to her room and be with her.

It was a house where she suffered bereavement, while she lived on herself into 1890. In 1883 Cayley died. She had seen him quite often in the eighteen years since she had refused him. They had exchanged tokens and letters. It was characteristic of him to send her a sea mouse, preserved in spirit, like her to love the gift, and write a little poem about it. His sudden death struck her a wounding blow. When she came to tell William Michael about it, he wrote: 'I shall not easily forget the look on her face, and the strain of self-command in her voice; she did not break down. She went to buy a wreath of flowers for him, and going to his rooms laid it upon the sheet.' A little while after his death she paid a solitary visit to his grave at Hastings, and wrote for him:

> Unmindful of the roses,
> Unmindful of the thorn,
> A reaper tired reposes
> Among his gathered corn:
> So might I till the morn.
>
> Cold as the cold Decembers,
> Past as the days that set,
> While only one remembers,
> And all the rest forget,—
> But one remembers yet.

Her mother died in 1886, and that was a loss of a different sort. Christina had lavished loved on her, love that she could give without any qualm or question. There was a calm steadfastness about Mrs Rossetti which had comforted the tempest-tossed Christina. There had been religious companionship which she could not get from William Michael, or Gabriel, perhaps not even from Maria with her overmastering certainties. Her 1882 Valentine to her mother gives us just this sense of comfort.

> My blessed mother dozing in her chair
> On Christmas day seemed an embodied Love,
> A comfortable love with soft brown hair
> Softened and silvered to a tint of dove;
> A better sort of Venus with an air
> Angelical from thoughts that dwell above;
> A wiser Pallas in whose body fair
> Enshrined a blessed soul looks out thereof.

It was natural, of course, for the mother to die, but again Christina is left to a solitary charge. With her usual humbleness she writes to William Michael: 'Please do not fancy me bearing this bitter trial better than I really am bearing it.'

But she was quite sure that she was in the right place however much she may have longed in some ways for the cool green house of her early dreams 'Full of sweet scents', and with the 'clear stream and the mossy stone.' No, she can write in 1888 to her brother: 'I yet am well content in my shady crevice; which crevice enjoys the unique advantage of being to my certain knowledge the place assigned to me.'

Two more volumes of poetry belong to the Torrington Square period. A *Pageant of Months and other poems* took its name from a Pageant that the All Saints sisters persuaded Christina to write for one of their occasions. Christina was no dramatist, her *Pageant* has been acted, but it is as a poem that it pleases us most. Here is April speaking:

Birth means dying
As wings and wind mean flying,
So you and I and all things fly or die
And sometimes I sit sighing to think of dying;
But meanwhile I've a rainbow for my showers
And a lap full of flowers—

She had what she called a 'quiet grin' at her self-portrait as
November, when October announces:

Here comes my younger sister looking dim
And grim.

The most important things in the book were the two sonnet
sequences *Monna Innominata* and *Later Life*. Gabriel Rossetti
lived just long enough to tell Christina how good he thought
they were. He was dying all that year, and Christina and her
mother were often in his house. Watts Dunton remembers the
extraordinary sense of light and peace when they were in the
house.

The last poem in her new volume tells again of the relationship of the Saviour to the saved which she never ceased to sing.

I have not sought Thee, I have not found Thee,
I have not thirsted for Thee:
And now cold billows of death surround me,
Buffeting billows of death astound me,——
    Wilt Thou look upon, wilt Thou see
    Thy perishing me?

Yea, I have sought thee, yea I have found thee,
Yea I have thirsted for thee,
Yea long ago with love's bands I bound thee:
Now the Everlasting Arms surround thee,
    Through death's darkness I look and see
    And clasp thee to Me.

The other book was the little poems collected out of her prose works, from *Time Flies* and *Called to the Saints*, and published by S.P.C.K. This book called *Verses* was very much beloved; it was published only two years before her death, and she was much cheered by the way it was received.

Christina's life was not entirely given to writing. For a long time she was an associate of a home for what the Victorians knew as 'fallen girls', and she writes that she is going to spend some weeks there only stipulating that she shall have time to correct some proofs. Mrs Bell Scott found her there once and wrote: 'On Wednesday we went to the top of Highgate Hill, where is the St Mary Magdalene home. Christina is now an associate, and wore a dress which is very simple, elegant even, black with hanging sleeves, a muslin cap with lace edging, quite becoming to her with the veil.'

She was one of the early opponents of vivisection, and collected signatures for an appeal against it. Womens' Suffrage, for which Adelaide Anne Proctor tried to enlist her sympathy left her rather disapproving, but admitting that: 'I do think if anything ever does sweep away the barrier of Sex, and make the female not a giantess or a heroine but at once and full grown a hero and a giant, it is that mighty maternal love which makes little birds and little beasts as well as little women matches for big adversaries.' But her brother says that she had no politics, and yet she was sensitive to the sufferings of the poor people. 'Alas, England, full of luxuries, and thronged by stinted poor!' she cries in one of her books, and in a letter writes: 'It is heart sickening to think of the terrible want of work and want of food at our doors, and we so comfortable.' William Michael says that she always gave away more money than she had to give, she was never unaware of need and suffering.

Christina was no recluse; she had always been in touch with interesting people, though her shyness and her silence made her sometimes a secret member of a group, she had a way of breaking her silence with a rather pregnant word, that caught the imagination of her hearers. Through Dante Gabriel she had known in her girlhood the members of the P.R.B. and also Madox Browne, Burne Jones, and William and Janie Morris; the life at Kelmscott was a happy part of her experience. Gosse, Watts Dunton, Swinburne, Bell Scott were all in her circle, and loved her work. Swinburne especially had a deep admiration for it. Of women writers, she knew and appreciated Jean Ingelow, Dora Greenwell and Adelaide Anne Proctor, a faithful friend till her death. Mrs Cameron, the photographer, loved her and her mother, and Lewis Carroll photographed them together. Among painters perhaps her closest friend was Frederick Shields who often discussed his work with her, and to whom she wrote a little note on her deathbed; Arthur Hughes, who illustrated her *Sing Song*, was another artist whose work she loved.

Through the restricted years in Torrington Square her friends did not desert her. They came to the house and found her in the first floor drawing room, her own special domain with two big windows looking out on to the Square garden, with the portraits by Dante Gabriel of various members of the family, and a reproduction of Shield's Good Shepherd, and a cut-glass chandelier which Gabriel had given to their mother and which glinted in the sunlight. Ford Maddox Hueffer describes her there as a 'black-robed figure, with clear-cut olive features, dark hair, and restrained formal gestures, her hands folded on her lap, her head judicially a little on one side' . . . a rather severe picture, for she said of herself, 'I was a very melancholy girl, now I am a cheerful old woman.'

Perhaps a more sympathetic description was given by Miss Lisa Wilson, much younger than Christina, who became very intimate with her in her last decade. Lisa Wilson describes herself as an 'invalidish' girl who wrote to Christina first to thank her for her poems. When Miss Wilson came to London, Christina was about to send her a copy of *Time Flies*, but she asked if she might come and receive the gift from its author's hands. 'Fetch it if you like', replied Christina, 'but don't expect me to be as nice as my poems, or you will be disappointed.' So they met and Miss Wilson saw 'a figure of medium height, with a sad set face, occasionally irradiated by a wonderful smile . . . she spoke gravely and quietly in her beautiful bell-like voice with sometimes a trace of gentle irony.' So Miss Sanders records Miss Wilson's recollection of the meeting. To the shy girl she became 'in truth my dearest friend and spiritual mother.'

Anyone who has been trusted by a younger friend in this way will know what this friendship meant to Christina, who wrote more intimately to this new friend than to anyone else, and saw her constantly till her death. She had another young friend whom she never saw, but who became a rather peculiar charge to her in her last years. This was Miss Newsham who was too ill to come to London, a girl who wrote poems herself, and was bold enough to write to Miss Rossetti to thank her for the comfort her poems had brought, and to ask for advice about publishing, and for criticism of her own poems. And she got both. For with great patience and tact Christina criticized her work. Perhaps it was a work of piety in memory of Gabriel's advice on her own work, for she wrote to this girl: 'My brother did in old days so much of the same kind for my poems, and they came out so much the better for his care. I like to imitate him in my turn, and here I am at your service.' Pretty good for the woman who was considered as a possible Poet Laureate! The poems never found their way to a publisher, but that does not mean that they were not interesting to Christina; or it may have been sheer pity for the ailing girl that dictated some thirty letters that she wrote to cheer her.

'Really', she wrote once, 'I find my condemned London trees cheerful. I hope you feel the same about your moon, stars, sunshine, remote country.' And again in spite of her own poor health and the charge of two ailing old aunts she repeats what she had said to William Michael: 'I am exactly where I should choose to abide, were the whole world open to my choice.' No, her crevice was not a prison, and it gave her the security of an absolutely obvious duty, and the hiddenness which is one of the secrets of the Kingdom of Heaven.

So the exchange of letters went on between them; sometimes Miss Newsham sent flowers from the country, once a photograph of herself of which Christina wrote characteristically, 'So now I have seen my friend's face, I hope at a future day I shall see it again, all glorious, and without a look of suffering.'

In 1892 Christina confided to William Michael that it might be necessary for her to have an operation for cancer. . . . 'But dear William do not worry yourself about me . . . come what will I am in Better Hands than yours or my own; I desire to realize and rest in this.' William came to her, and saw her through the operation which was successful for the time. She was sent down to Brighton to recover, and wrote from there to Lucy Rossetti: 'One of my occupations is to lie down, another is to write letters, another is to go out in a chair. Shall I reckon breakfasting in bed as an occupation?'

Later she could write to Miss Newsham: 'I am brisk, writing

to you with ease and pleasure', and to William, 'I go on, if not friskily, doggedly.'

Verses came out at this point, and she did enjoy hearing how much people were appreciating them. All the same she was rather horrified when in the same year her name was proposed as Poet Laureate after Tennyson's death. 'She shuddered', wrote Ford Madox Hueffer 'at the suggestion', and she taxed him with exaggerating the rumour.

The last charge ended when old Miss Eliza Polidori died in 1893. Christina's care of these old ladies, one of them quite senile, had been undertaken so much as a matter of course, and with such quiet charity and affection, that perhaps one is inclined to miss all that it meant of expenditure of strength and energy. Her sympathy must have been going out all this time to William, for Lucy Rossetti was desperately ill, going from place to place with her devoted daughters, in search of health, while William worked on for the family in London. She died in the April of 1894 at San Remo. So now just the brother and sister were left of the brilliant family, and Christina was dying. Her bed was moved into her drawing room, and there she could still see some friends; and in October, William found her quite gay, remembering old nonsense verses they had made, and putting him right about memories of their childhood that he needed for a memoir he was making of Dante Gabriel. But after that it was a sad month or two till she died. Long strain, and duty performed above her strength took its revenge, and she was often in the deeps, sure that she could never reach that Heaven of her poems, she was too wicked, and unfit. 'All Thy waves and storms have gone over me', she might have said. The valley of the shadow of death was long for her, but at the end of it she did reach a peace of heart. Liza Wilson who knew her so well felt that her glooms were simply part of her illness, for 'her love and trust in God's mercy were infinite.' She was murmuring quiet prayers, not noticing anything that went on around on those last days, but praying till within five minutes of her death.

Light is our sorrow for it ends tomorrow,
    Light is our death which cannot hold us fast;
So brief a sorrow can be scarcely sorrow,
    Or death so quickly past.

One night, no more, of pain that turns to pleasure,
    One night, no more of weeping, weeping sore;
And then the heaped up measure beyond measure,
    In quietness for evermore.

EDWARD KING

1829—1910

WHERE can they be going these young men, groping along a garden path by dim lamp light in the precincts of Christchurch, Oxford, some time in the spring of 1876? It might be a meeting of a secret society, for there is no lecture-room at the end of the garden, only an uncouth building, wash-house, brewhouse. . . . What is the attraction? They push the door open, and crowd in, fill up the chairs and wait. There is light enough to see, a faldstool, a picture and a harmonium, at which one of them goes to officiate. But as the great clock in Tom Tower begins to strike eight, there is a familiar heavy tread, and there enters, clad in a rather crumpled surplice, the man who has attracted them to this unusual meeting-place. All eyes were focused on Edward King, at this time Professor of Pastoral Theology at Oxford. 'It was light', wrote Scott Holland, 'that he carried with him, light that flowed from him. The room was lit into which he entered . . . those eyes of his were an illumination. Even to recall him for an instant in the bare memory was enough to set all the day alive and glittering.'

Edward King had made this 'little Bethel', when his hearers grew too many for any room in his house. 'Last term' (he wrote), 'I started a little Bethel in my garden, it was a wash-house, and we cleaned it out, and put coconut matting and chairs and a

harmonium, very simple but very lovely. We had a sort of
meditation every Friday night at eight p.m. I enjoyed it immensely . . . poor things they were so good, the place was
crammed.' Edward King's genius for loving God, and loving
men had a magnetic quality. That genius was lodged in an
extraordinarily humble heart. Humbleness and love together
produced a rare kind of entirely natural holiness, very strong,
highly disciplined, but not in the least forced.

He had had rather a sheltered childhood; he was the third
child in the big family of his parson father; he was delicate, and
never went to school, and so perhaps some of the bloom of
childhood stayed with him. But quite early he had made the
acquaintance of suffering, watching by the bed of his invalid
sister Anne, with whom he often sat up all night.

His father was a parson of a very old-fashioned type. Many
people will remember the story of how, having asked Edward
if he knew his Catechism, he sent him riding off to be confirmed
in a nearby parish with no more ado, or preparation. His
mother seems to have had some of that brightness and wisdom
that characterized her son. I should like to know more about his
tutor John Day who must have laid some pretty firm foundations of Tractarian teaching, and with whom Edward spent his
terms till he went up to Oxford in 1848 to Oriel.

He was not at all effeminate, this strikingly beautiful young
man; he was a superb horseman, fond of dancing, fishing, and
swimming. 'A royal fellow', said his much-loved tutor Charles
Marriott. But through his Oxford life runs the sharp steel of
discipline. 'I observe, Mr King', said the austere Provost
Hawkins of Oriel, 'that you have never missed a single chapel,
morning or evening, during the whole term', and proceeded to
give him a warning against formalism. He need not have

troubled; no one's religion sprang so spontaneously from the heart as King's, but he kept the vigils and fasts of the Church too, and absented himself from Hall on Fast days.

Charles Marriot was Oriel's best gift to King, who called him 'the most Gospel-minded man I ever knew.' Marriott who had been Newman's disciple till his going over to Rome, who with Keble and Pusey had compiled the Library of the Fathers, had all the graciousness of the Oxford Movement, and all its staunch adherence in the glory of the Church to give to his young friend. What we know of King's Oriel period, does not show us that he had that overwhelming influence over young men there, that came to him later, though he was generally loved and esteemed in the college. He left Oxford in 1852, and made a pilgrimage to the Holy Land which he felt all his life to have been of the greatest importance.

After a short time as a private tutor, he came to the time of his Ordination, and so came to be curate of Wheatley. Wheatley and Cuddesdon lie in the same district a little to the east of Oxford. They were both to be important in his story. Mr Elton, his first vicar at Wheatley, had just lost his wife, and felt that he could not go on struggling with a very tough and wild parish without someone to support and help him. Writing many years after, he said of King: 'He was everything to me.' King came to live at the vicarage with the vicar and his motherless children. Elton was surprised to find how much his curate knew about prayer, and the Bible, perhaps most of all how much he cared about the boys in the parish, whose reputation had not been encouraging, how ready he was for the fight with bad conditions and the unsavoury character of the place. And it was all done with such cheer and grace, with that same sort of radiance which was to fascinate people all his life long. The motherless children at the parsonage loved him, and he took them out bird-nesting and found them flowers, which he always loved. But it was the farm boys in that country parish who drew out of him his characteristic response to their need. 'These rough carter lads' (he wrote) 'need to be surrounded by a flame of love.'

A flame of love was what he gave to them; he surrounded them with this heavenly warmth of affection, and they took to dropping in to talk to him over the fire in his room, they would carry him almost up the steep hills when his heart was troubling him. They knew that there was nothing that he didn't know about their own job of caring for horses, and that he was a superb rider, and something that he was giving them made them feel that he could mount them too, and ride away with them into a country new to their wild young hearts. They discovered that suffering and death didn't daunt him when they saw him nursing the worst cases in a typhus epidemic that broke out in the ill-drained village. They followed him into Church because they could understand what he was talking about there, and could watch him as he prayed, and begin to worship too.

They must have felt how much he enjoyed being curate at Wheatley; indeed to the end of his life King had a sort of nostalgia for Wheatley. 'I don't know that I have ever been happier' (he wrote forty years later to one of his boys). 'I was thoroughly happy with you all at Wheatley. . . . It was very nice, wasn't it? I hope you are able to keep the same spirit of simplicity and love round about you.'

Wilberforce, Bishop of Oxford, had launched an important experiment in his Theological College at Cuddesdon. It was under his own eye there, as his Bishop's Palace was nearby, and the Principal of the College was also vicar of the parish of Cuddesdon. But he found it a little worrying to get just the right staff. The College was rather suspect with the Low Church folk, and altogether as the Principal later told King they wanted 'a change of tone'. The Curate from Wheatley had been to preach at Cuddesdon once or twice, and it seemed to Wilberforce that he might be just the right man to be Chaplain at the Theological College. This was surely a man to give the students there the highest ideals for their vocation.

King hesitated to leave his beloved Wheatley, but after a decisive meeting with his Bishop, King leaning against a stile and the Bishop on horseback, the Bishop's final word, as he kicked his horse and rode off: 'Well, I think you ought to go', clinched the matter and he became Chaplain of Cuddesdon, to try his flame of love with quite a different type of man from his ploughboys at Wheatley. The magnetism of his love again had an extraordinary effect, and the bunch of letters from his young men that was handed to his first biographer, show that breaking down of barriers, that assurance of the Chaplain's care for all sides of their lives, their souls, their families, their homes, their cricket matches. . . . 'Everything', says Russell, 'breathes the most affectionate feeling for the Chaplain, the warmest gratitude for good gained at Cuddesdon, and a singularly keen sense of brotherhood'.

When the Principal died rather suddenly, King succeeded him, also becoming Vicar of Cuddesdon, and began ten years of remarkable work.

There never was anything else quite so full of thrill (wrote Scott Holland) as the old days on the blessed hill when King was Principal. The whole place was alive with him; his look, his voice, his gaiety, his beauty, his charm and his holiness filled it and possessed it. He grew happier and happier, his eyes twinkled with dauntless merriment, his presence beamed with joy.

But that was not to say that the flame of love did not light King into the darkest places of men's hearts.

'Our only course', wrote one of his men, 'was to submit our lives, our difficulties, our temptations and sins, hopes and fears, to one who seemed to know them all without needing to be told.' 'It was a new experience to find a man full of such affectionate interest in our individual spiritual welfare', wrote another. 'We were most tenderly, yet unflinchingly compelled to face our lives before God. Until now we had never understood ourselves.'

King himself wrote of those Cuddesdon years:

Cuddesdon was a place where I spent fourteen of the happiest years of my life, receiving kindnesses and blessings which I can never repay; and yet after all it was not the place, but the teaching, the life, that made Cuddesdon so dear to us. There we lived in the daily enjoyment of the friendship of English hearts, strengthened, softened, perfected by the full power of the whole Catholic Church. Cuddesdon has been and is one of our best defences against infidelity, and Rome. Her students have not sought money or patronage from the world; one thing they have desired . . . liberty to tell the poor 'the whole counsel of God'.

The Principal of Cuddesdon was also vicar of the parish, so that he did get there that contact with poor people which was always so precious to him. He used to keep Friday nights free for his people to come and visit him. One Friday night, going out late into his garden he discovered a young man who had been trying for three hours to summon up courage to come in to see him. He used to say of his farm labourers, 'They are very ignorant, have very little time, work very hard, and often with poor food. They require a great deal of loving watchful sympathy.'

One thing he had to give to them, a very simple way of talking of holy things. His sermons could be understood by all, and yet wise people found a real depth in them. The congregation at Evensong in Cuddesdon Church was a wonderful mixture: his own students, their friends out from Oxford, the Bishop and his guests at the Palace, his farmer friends (who, by the way, had all become communicants), and then the labourers and their wives. They loved to remember that he had something for them all.

His was a practical friendship too; he gave his own riding horse to a parishioner who had lost his horse, and when a small-pox epidemic broke out in the parish, he rushed back from his holidays to tend the worst cases, actually laying out the dead when no one else would touch them.

One of King's most dear friends at Cuddesdon was Stephen Gladstone, son of the Prime Minister, and it was he perhaps who suggested to his father, when the Chair of Pastoral Theology fell vacant at Oxford, that King would be the man to fill it. True, he had left Oxford without any particular academic distinction, as critics in Oxford were not slow to point out, but on the other hand who had proved himself to know more about Pastoral Theology? So the offer was made and accepted, to the agonizing grief of the Cuddesdon students who choked down their sobs when King announced his decision; and King went to live in Christchurch taking with him his mother, now a widow, who seemed to add her own brightness and grace to the atmosphere of the house. A chill had fallen on the Church at Oxford at that time; Pusey was old and very deaf and coming near to the end of his life. He and King had the most affectionate relationship, and King had in past years made his first Confession to Pusey; Jowett was brilliant but not warm. The flame of love was

needed there as elsewhere, and King's vital conception of the
meaning of Pastoral Theology affected many more young men
than those reading Theology who were his first care. 'Hungry
sheep looked up' and were fed. They came to his lectures,
to his house, to Bethel. They flocked to hear him preach, and
went away stirred and satisfied.

There were storms on the sea of religion nearly all the time
that King was at Oxford, but King had a sort of serenity of heart
that rode them without dismay. He was, he confessed at first,
very frightened of going to learned Oxford, but he soon knew
why he was there. He didn't neglect the controversies of his
time, and he spent a long vacation in Germany improving his
German so that he could study German critical writing. When
the Public Worship Regulation Act, which Disraeli tersely
called 'a Bill to put down Ritualism' was passed, he wrote:

> The speeches in Parliament and Convocation have been very try-
> ing and disappointing. . . . Evidently the people are not yet won to
> Church Principles. I confess I was longing for rest too soon. We
> must turn to again, and teach in the quiet early Tractarian way.
> That seems the thing to do. Not to lose heart, or get hard with dis-
> appointment; but to get a help in Humility, feeling that Parlia-
> ment does not like us or want us and to set to work again with
> individuals in the clear and healthy atmosphere of Unpopularity.

So he set to work to make saints for his Church. Writing to his
sister he said: 'I want to see English saints made in the old way,
by suffering and labour, and diligence in little things, and the
exercise of unselfish untiring Love. Do let us try to rear a few
quiet English saints.'

1877 was a particularly turbulent year: Russo-Turkish War,
the Public Worship Regulation Bill, strikes all over England,
but King wrote to one of his old students working abroad:

In all this I have not myself suffered, nor yet been inwardly disturbed. There is nothing that I see to shake the principles of one's inner life. This last Confession panic will in the end do good; when people get quiet again they will see (1st) that there is such a thing as Absolution—(2nd) that the natural act of confession is not taken from them by the supernatural gift of pardon. Then they will use their liberty as they need. These disturbances are, I feel, bringing forward into view great truths which we have more or less neglected.

And he writes to one of the young men whom he had trained:

It is a very great pleasure to me to think of you all at work. There is a very great opportunity for you. I'm sure we must all be full of hope, brave, self-sacrificing, victorious hope. To me, thank God, all these troubles of the intellect, and all our ecclesiastical and social anxieties are full of life. They are but, I believe, the pain and labour which will issue in the birth of more truth, more true liberty, more true union between Man and Nature, and Man and God, a bringing us in all things nearer to Him. Only, dearest child, in all this we must keep quiet and steady in our personal unity with Him.

And again:

I do value so highly a natural growth in holiness, a humble grateful acceptance of the circumstances that God has provided for us, and I dread the unnatural, cramped, ecclesiastical holiness, which is so much more quickly produced, but is so human and poor.

It was Gladstone who offered the Bishopric of Lincoln to King in 1885; in doing this he enriched the office of a bishop by the choice of a man whose holiness was unquestioned, and whose love for God and man was at full flow. Since the day of Thomas Ken there had not been an English Diocesan who was so clearly a saint.

He said a touching farewell to his listeners in Bethel, first of all asking their pardon and God's pardon for all the ways in which he had failed them, and then thanking God for upholding his faith while he had been in Oxford. 'I leave Oxford restful, thankful, and as a believer.' Then he asked them to strive for Personal Communion with God both in faith and life, and he asked to aim high in their lives. 'It is quite possible to stay at the bottom on the smooth level ground; the timid one dares not to climb lest he fall. But it is the invitation of the Holy Spirit, 'Friend, come up higher'. It is not ambition. There is detachment provided for you as you go on, if you will go on.'

Two final laws of the spiritual life he gave them: Remember the Law of Suffering, and remember the Law of Handing On to younger men lines of thought, footprints, etc., to step in.

'Brothers, dear brothers', he ended, 'I have had to speak roughly to you tonight, just as Joseph spoke roughly to his brothers—for fear of breaking down.'

Possibly his appointment as Bishop of Lincoln was in a way a release, and that Oxford had rather cramped his style.

Now I am to go back to the care of souls (he wrote) and be shepherd again of the sheep and lambs.

I have as you know no great gifts, he wrote to a fellow Canon of Christ Church, but by God's goodness, I have a real and great love of His poor. If it should please Him to let me be the Bishop of His poor, and enable them to see more what they are to Him, and what He is to them, I think I shall be very happy.

'It shall be a bishopric of love', wrote Scott Holland to him, discerning his real genius, and so indeed it was.

Lincoln was just the right Diocese for his particular gifts, with its multitude of little country parishes (plenty of ploughboys) suffering a good deal at that time from a period of agricultural depression, its clergy rather discouraged and very hard up, its county people staunch and loyal.

The magnetism of his love and simplicity and holiness worked

116

once more. 'He is adored in Lincoln', wrote his contemporary, Archbishop Benson. Scott Holland remembered: 'Twice I went down with him to Lincoln Fair, all among the coconuts, and the gingerbread, and the fat women; it was a delicious experience to note the affection that followed him about. He drew out love, as the sun draws fragrance from flowers.' Indeed it is noteworthy that King not only gave love but made other people loving.

'From the porters at Lincoln Station', writes Lord Elton, 'who would whisper eagerly: 'The Bishop's here . . .', to the Master of Foxhounds who kept only two photographs on his table, one of his favourite hound, and the other of the Bishop, the Diocese was at his feet.'

And yet marvellously he kept his humility inviolate, and they noticed that too, these Lincolnshire people. 'I would mention first his intense humility', said one, and it certainly glints through his letters.

Do pray for better bishops. These people might be angels and archangels straight off, if we were only decent.

I think I have begun to see my way to the alphabet of morality, but I have hardly begun Christianity, and I was fifty-four last Saturday.

One cannot help feeling almost a desire to be hung or shot, instead of being buried as if one was good.

This, dear child, is what I want you to get—that you should increase in self-hating reverence for others, and grow in the general apprehension that others are a few million times better than oneself, and only to be interfered with with awe.

I am off to China by the first boat! Will you come? I've just come back from a meeting where a beautiful C.M.S. missionary straight from China has been preaching—at least what I call preaching—talking the Gospel with all the fervour of a living missionary. Most crushing! Eleven years and no results, and five deaths! Then three converts! Then another death! Then another year, and then

7000. And such beauties. My dear child, if ever you or I get just in, it will only be by holding on to the extremest tip of one of their pigtails——

One of whom I felt quite unworthy who died a felon's death in goal.

This love which was poured out on him it was his great desire to offer to Christ. He wrote to one of his students: 'You must take care to draw him by your heart to God, and not to yourself. It is heartbreaking work, but God will help you if you give yourself to Him.'

In one of his pastoral Theology lectures he tells his hearers that their aim with their people must be 'not only to win them, but to guide them into holiness.' But people must see holiness before they want it, and what King presented to his Lincolnshire people was this very holiness, this sense of a man transfigured by his Communion with God. 'To see him pass down the aisle of the Church was a benediction. As soon as I saw him in the pulpit I felt I wanted to be good, and I knew I could be. I was confirmed by him just 62 years ago, and I still remember his lovely voice and beautiful face. Do they always send a saint from heaven to confirm you?' These were things that ordinary people in Lincolnshire said of him.

I am not very old yet, but I have seen enough of bodily and mental suffering', he said to his clergy when he came to the Diocese, and he was ready, as only a saint can be, to enter into the sufferings of others.

When he was still at Oxford he had written to one of his young men who was struggling in an ungrateful post:

I am sorry you are so squeezed, but it must be so more or less. Anyone who has a high ideal, and love of perfection must be prepared to suffer.

I am so sorry for you, and yet it must be or you would not be worth your salt in such a place. Only by breaking your heart to pieces over and over again can you hope to make them begin to think of believing that there is such a thing as love.

And to another, later, at Lincoln: 'Any kind of public life must be self-sacrifice. "He saved others, himself he cannot save" is true of all who would try to follow Him. Smashing is in the bond, though it may not be exacted to the full.'

For his discouraged and lonely clergy he had the deepest care and affection, understanding, and suffering with them, and offering them some of the rare joys they had ever experienced. He invited them to come into Retreat once a year with him in the Cathedral, and the first of these Retreats, that he himself took in 1890, made a very deep impression, for to many it was the beginning of a new kind of Christian life. A parson who was there wrote: 'What renewal of hopes, what possibilities were before us! We had seen it all. We had a bishop and a friend, a father who knew and understood.' He cared also for their circumstances: and entered into the straits of the Agricultural depression with real costly sympathy.

We have suffered dreadfully here from agricultural distress (he wrote in 1888). . . . I have never been so distressed about money as I have been since I have been a bishop. The clergy cannot live. What are we to do?

'He came like a good angel of hope and encouragement', says George Russell, 'to the isolated parishes in the fens and the wolds, cheering disheartened clergymen, and preaching to the labourers in language they could understand. Though he taught in its fullness the Catholic interpretation of the Faith, he so phrased his teaching that the stiffer Church folk regarded him as 'nowt but an old Methody'; and an enthusiastic visitor from the Salvation Army declared: 'It might have been the General himself.'

Again his gift of understanding young boys made his Confirmation addresses memorable. There was one depressed parson who felt that his boys were not making a preparation for their Easter Communion, and complained to King that all his enquiries had got from one of them was that he had cleaned his best shoes, and put them under his bed. 'Well', said King, 'don't you think the angels must be very glad to see them there?'

There was one special kind of suffering which he embraced with deep love and humility. A young Grimsby fisherman who had murdered his sweetheart was condemend to death at the Lincoln Assizes. The prison Chaplain felt that the burden of preparing him for death was more than he could carry, and King stepped in to help him. He found that the young man had no knowledge of the Christian Faith, had scarcely heard of God. There was only a short time, but King began to teach him about sin, death and forgiveness, using the Parable of the Prodigal Son. In those short weeks, the man was confirmed, made his confession, and before his death received the Holy Communion. King went with him to the scaffold, sustaining him to the end.

There were other times later when the Bishop visited those who were condemned to death. Of one of these he wrote to a friend: 'You will have seen I daresay that we are in trouble here again. A poor dear Grimsby fisherman. It will be over, a fortnight tomorrow. Will you please remember him and ask that he may be forgiven and accepted, and for me that my sins may not hinder me from helping him.'

A little of the cost is revealed in the next sentence. 'I am just back from the gaol, so my hand shakes, but not for him.'

But if he was prepared to suffer, and knew that only by suffering could he get communion with the Lord, he was also an adept at rejoicing. All his life long he rejoiced in natural things, flowers, birds, and all growing things. Towards the end of his life he wrote: 'I go on in my simple superficial way, loving flowers, and birds, and the sunlight on the apples, and the sunset; and like to think more and more of that verse "With Thee is the well of life, and in Thy light shall we see light".'

And again: 'I hope to try and not let the wear of life rub off the bloom of a childlike happiness which I believe our Father would like to see us have.

'Nothing is so beautiful as the beauty of good people; it is most refreshing.'

He had always been one of the people to whom a holiday abroad brought the greatest delight. Switzerland was his paradise, but he loved also to be in Italy.

He could be a very lighthearted letter writer: 'By all means be my chaplain on the 22nd and save me from scandalizing all the little acolytes by not bowing and bending as they would wish. I shall feel safe in your hands, as I know there is no kind of degree of good or evil of that sort to which you are not equal—you naughty, wicked James.'

The big house at Riseholme had been sold, and the Old Palace, Lincoln, became his home. It lay under the Cathedral heights, and from it he could look out over the wide spaces of his diocese. Its chapel, so dear to so many people, had been furnished mainly by his friends, as a gift of love to him.

Something must be said about his hospitality at the Old Palace, which varied from retreats for his clergy and ordinands, to an annual dinner, to the jockeys riding in the Lincoln Handicap. Here is what one lay friend though about it.

For thirty years that priceless gift was ours; throughout that time it was a well spring of pure joy to us to be near him in Holy

Week, or on his holidays abroad, to rejoice in his constant thought and care for those about him, from the lad who carried the coal-scuttles to the most honoured of his guests. . . . From the first of these blessed visits to the last, it was ever the same bright welcome, the same tender thoughtfulness, the same helpful smile and word of encouragement and solace.

And what about the other people who lived in the Old Palace, his household, quite a large Victorian one? 'The Old Palace was a happy home for us', said his housekeeper, and she went on to say how appreciative the Bishop was of good work. Every Friday evening when he was at home he spoke to them in the chapel. He remembered to bring them each a present when he went on holiday. On his eightieth birthday he gave them each a framed photograph of himself, and they in return gave him a hat and gloves. Such were the terms that made the Old Palace a happy home. Once a year his butler presented him with all outstanding bills, and when these had been paid the balance was given away to those in need of help.

But goodness is always liable to attack, and perhaps the most bitter attacks come not from evil, but from near goodness.

When King was made Bishop of Lincoln there had been a certain amount of protest against what the protesters called the Romish tendency of the Bishop's thought. Did he not belong to the E.C.U.? Was there not a display of gaudy geegaws at his enthronement? Somehow this all fell rather flat in the Diocese which was beginning to understand the spiritual stature of its Bishop. 'Lincolnshire knew that it had got a saint, and was serenely indifferent to his garb, gestures and postures', wrote George Russell. But a society called the Church Association pursued the attack. It had caused quite a few priests to be imprisoned. Why not fly for higher game? Why not see if Archbishop Benson could be forced to cite and try the Bishop of Lincoln?

The Romish practices, the points on which the Bishop was attacked, were the Eastward Position during the prayer of Consecration, lights on the altar, the mixture of water and wine in the chalice, the Agnus Dei sung after the Consecration, the use of the sign of the Cross at the Absolution and Blessing, and the Ablution of the sacred vessels. It is hard to think ourselves back seventy years and to see how these things appeared to the Church Association as leading directly to Rome, knowing that now in most Anglican churches they are part of the order and very much part of the character of Anglican worship to-day.

King was not at all Romish in his beliefs, and always rather unhappy about the wild extremes to which some of the High Church parsons had allowed themselves to adopt; he used these practices for greater devotion and inspiration of his people. If we are looking to him for sanctity, we shall find it especially in his passionate desire that the Will of God may be done, as the outcome of this attack on himself, and a strange trustful serenity which came to him in all these troubles:

> I cannot help thinking (he wrote to one of his Chapter) that the good Archbishop would have been supported, and saved great trouble if he had felt able to refuse to entertain the charges from the first. But God may have greater blessings for us than we see. Thank God, I have not been worried about the matter yet. My one anxiety and daily prayer is that I may do His Will.

To an old Cuddesdon friend he wrote: 'Just now the water is a little rough,' but I trust all will end for the good of the Church.'

1888 was the Lambeth Conference year, and when one of the

American bishops asked King to come to America for a visit in the next year he was astounded when King answered quite calmly that he might very likely be in prison at that time.

But there was a long time of tension to be lived through. After much questioning, the Archbishop decided that he could try the case himself at Lambeth, at a court held in his Library there. King and his supporters asked that like other Englishmen he should be tried by his peers, his fellow-bishops, but he nevertheless answered the summons under protest. There followed months of delay in which Benson with a good deal of integrity prepared his judgment, which was not given until two years after the attack began.

But one thing of real value did come to the Church during those months of waiting. There was a great wave of prayer, not that this or that should be decided, but, as King had longed, that God's will might be done. 'You may be sure', wrote Fr Benson, superior of the S.S.J.E., 'that any difficulties which you may have to meet are fully compensated for by the spirit of prayer aroused in so many throughout the land.'

And it was so. King was so beloved that in cathedrals and parish churches, ruridecanal chapters, convents, and groups of clergy not only in England, but wherever the Church of England was alive all over the world, came not only expressions of sympathy, but promises of prayer, asking for God's guidance to the Archbishop and for Peace for King himself. Evangelicals, and high churchmen alike were sending messages of prayer and understanding love. And King, whose first action was to pay a friendly visit to the man who had mainly instigated the attack, did attain to the Peace which passes understanding.

There were those who actually reviled him in letters and speeches, but he never answered them. He did feel the support of the prayers to be the most real help. He wrote to the subdean of Lincoln, Clements:

> I am sure I owe you with others more than I can say for the support you have gained for me through prayer during this past year, for I have been most mercifully upheld, with hardly any suffering, though of course the special burden is a great and unexpected one. . . . Something of the sort, I think was probably necessary, and it is a wonderful mercy that it has come in a way which causes no ill-feeling towards anyone, and has not hindered the general work of the Dioceses.

It was in fact an enheartening example of how a time of tension and strain may be faced without bitterness and in expectation of a blessing.

For the judgment did bring some real gains to the Church apart from the main value of perceiving that these things could be faced without ill-feeling.

King's dignified letter to his clergy shows his own feeling of thankfulness.

> The following points appear to me to demand especial thankfulness.
>
> 1st: that the judgment is based on independent enquiry, and that it recognizes the continuity of the Church.
>
> 2nd: that the Primitive and all but universal custom of administering a mixed cup in the Holy Eucharist has been preserved.
>
> 3rd: that the remaining elements may be reverently consumed by the cleansing of the vessels immediately after the close of the service.
>
> 4th: that it is allowable by the use of two lights, and of singing during the Celebration of Holy Communion to assist the devotions of our people.
>
> With regard to the Manual Acts I defer to the construction which His Grace has put upon the rubric.
>
> Similarly with regard to the use of the sign of the Cross in

pronouncing Absolution, and Benediction, I shall in deference to the ruling of His Grace no longer practice it.

While the points that have given in my favour are declared to be lawful, it is not intended that they should be obligatory. You, my Reverent Bretheren, are well aware that I have never desired to enforce unaccustomed ritual upon any reluctant clergyman or congregation.

At the same time, I earnestly hope that this authoritative utterance of our revered and beloved Archbishop will tend to remove the suspicion of lawlessness, and unfaithfulness to the Church of England, which has unhappily arisen in some places with regard to points of ceremonial observance. My prayer is that this judgment may be for the greater glory of God, and for the edification of our souls in unity and peace.

So graciously he accepted the judgment, and the Church was enriched by his obedience.

But he did emerge from this tension a frailer man physically. He had very much disliked the publicity. 'Perhaps a better and a braver man' (he wrote to a friend), 'would have rejoiced at fighting so good a cause; but my little experience has taught me that suffering is a very disturbing thing, and requires more grace than most of us possess.'

He gave himself again quietly to his pastoral work which he loved so much. He had once said that what he wanted to do was 'to draw men to Christ, that they might be nearer to God and nearer to each other in the unity of the Church.' Some things in the Diocese were especially dear to him. As was to be expected from the ex-Principal of Cuddesdon, the 'Scholae Cancellarii', the Theological College at Lincoln, was his constant care; so were the two Rescue Homes at Boston and Lincoln. He had a special concern for the men who worked on the railway, whom he saw so often as he moved about his Diocese by train, as bishops did in those days. He would cast a keen eye round a station on the lookout for friends, porters, drivers, clerks and guards; he remembered the porters at the little junctions where he had to change and asked after their families. He found out cases of hardship or illness from Inspectors or Guards, and often sent help to them. He was never busy when a railway man wanted to see him. 'What a fine body of men the railway system has created', he said, 'men who all over the country stand for courage, intelligence, sobriety, and courtesy.' He started a little guild for them, with the Michaelmas collect as their own prayer, and he used to visit them on Michaelmas day.

From Oxford days he had cherished the St Barnabas Guild for Nurses belonging to the Church. He used to write them a yearly letter of appreciation and counsel and he held the highest ideals for them as the following passage shows: 'It is your great work to bring the likeness and Mind and Spirit of Christ into the sickroom, into every ward in the Hospital, and into the mind and heart of every sick person in the Ward. Let this be your New Year's thought: "I am to carry on the great work of the Incarnation".'

His letters of counsel and spiritual direction were very simple and clear. Here is one to a priest, troubled about his faith:

I am very sorry that you have been in anxiety about your faith, but that, I believe, is often one of God's own ways of giving us discipline to train us for His great service. The suffering for the faith, and the fear of losing it often lead us to value it more really than when it is taken for granted without cost. The fact that you desire to believe the Truth is of priceless value, and please God will lead you on to full belief. Faith is the gift of God, and requires a general self-surrender on our part. Sometimes there are stiff bits in us which we hardly recognize as sin, but they prevent the perfect self-surrender and humility which is necessary. A German bishop (Sailer) for whom I have a grateful regard, puts it:

1. Self-surrender.
2. Acceptance.
3. Faith.

I sincerely hope and trust that if you persevere in humble prayer that in His good time after you have suffered a while, God will give you the blessing of Peace in Believing.

His letters to those who had lost people whom they loved are full of quiet strength. Here is one to a friend whose daughter had died:

Thank you for your great kindness in allowing me so quickly to be with you in your great sorrow, for so it must be, even to the most Christian heart. I had hoped and prayed that if it pleased God you might all be spared this great pain, but He who did not withdraw the Cup in the Garden knows what is best. On this we may most surely rest, and in time or in eternity we shall know this. At present we may not be able to do more than accept and believe it, but such acceptance is surely most blessed in its fruits, for it is the union of our will and His will, and this is the central point of the restoration of the Divine likeness in us, and our especial preparation for our eternal Communion in Heaven. Through suffering we are perfected.

And this to another:

A new nearness to God, a purer intention, a more direct living for the world beyond, a new freedom and sense of independence to the world, its frowns and smiles, a firmer courage, these, dear friend, are some of the gifts and consolations I believe you will find in God's good time.

One letter to a child gives us a rare picture of his humility and love:

I am so very sorry you have not had the peacock's feathers. It was not all my fault, as I told my butler when I got home to be sure and send them by the carrier, but he forgot, and I'm afraid I never asked him, as I might have done, whether he had sent them. However, I have told him to send them off by post today, so I hope you and Baby will have them ready for your hats on Easter Sunday. I hope your daffodils will make haste and come out for Easter too. The Spring is like the Resurrection; all the Winter things look dead, then in Spring they all rise up to life again. You should look at the buds on the trees, and see how wonderfully they are all packed up, so snug and safe until Winter is over, and then they just peep out, and then when the cold has gone, out they come, beautiful and wonderful! It shows us how great and how gentle God is. When you grow up to be a strong man you must remember always to be gentle . . .

I am, your affectionate old Bishop . . .

People came to trust his quiet unembittered judgment. When the Ritual troubles flared up again over incense and portable lights he guided his own Diocese to an almost unanimous obedience to the decisions of the two Archbishops. He felt more keenly about Reservation for the sick, and helped his own clergy to meet the need of invalids who had depended upon this. But like the early Tractarians he mistrusted mock-Romanism:

Some men (he wrote) have been adopting all kinds of medieval and modern Roman ways, for which there is really no sort of authority in the Church of England and in the Primitive Church. Now I hope we shall come back nearer to the true English Position of Holy Scripture and the Primitive Church. We need not be surprised if the zeal of the same young men carried them too far in the matter of Confession and Eucharistic Doctrine. I believe most of them will be willing to come back to the Church of England standard, and the young ones who are coming up can have the danger made plain to them. One loves the zeal and self-devotion of many of the men who have been led on too far: but some, I fear, are in danger of losing sight of the highest and most spiritual things, and becoming humanly Ecclesiastical.

Later he wrote to Archbishop Temple: 'As matters are going on, I believe in a few years the strength and weakness of Ritual will be better understood, and people better able to form a true judgment on the matter.'

In 1897 Temple asked him to conduct a quiet day for the Bishops assembled again for the Lambeth Conference. He pictured them simply coming as the Apostles came to Jesus, telling Him all things, 'both what they had done and what they had taught.'

This is a busy age, and bishops, thank God, are expected to work, and the danger perhaps, is of being over busy—doing too much, and forgetting the other account we have to render, of what we have taught. . . . The question arises how far have we for our own sakes, or for the sake of others, borne the heat and the burden of the day?

How far, since being made a bishop, has the pressure of the secular part of one's work, the ceaseless letters, the routine of business, and much that is exhausting, and yet that has little in it that is spiritual, taken away one's mind from higher things? How far since we were made bishops have we taken out due share in the intellectual and spiritual troubles of our own people? We may humbly hope that He who knows all things will look mercifully on the confusion and lowness of our present lives.

He went back to Oriel memories, and quoted Marriott's words which had inspired him so much as an undergraduate. 'Meditation on Christ, prayer to Him, learning of Him, conformity to Him, partaking of Him are the chief business of the Christian life.'

Then in his own words: 'The new social forces have been gaining great strength in late years. My fear is that some of us have not grown proportionately in the knowledge of our Lord and Saviour Jesus Christ. Some of us have been so occupied in securing the reality of morals that, I fear, we do not give to Christ the place which as Christians we should ascribe to him.'

And so he brought the bishops to the crux of their religion: union with Christ.

He was unhappy about the trend of education in the primary schools. None of the four bills that had been put forward had satisfied him that Church children were going to get Church teaching.

> During the last three years (he wrote) no less than four Education bills have failed . . . why is it that these efforts have failed? I believe it is because they contained elements that were not right; so they have been stopped. If the Government desire our co-operation they must propose some educational plan which we can accept with a good conscience.

He was growing old, and wondering very much how long he should hold on to the work of the See. He still enjoyed a holiday abroad in 1908 in Italy:

> This is a lovely little out-of-the-world place (he wrote from Abetone) 6,400 feet up in the Appenines most delicious air, and lovely restful scenery, not grand and terrible like Switzerland, but peaceful and suited for an old man of 78. . . . I hope you are having a holiday somewhere. It does one so much good, besides being so nice.

A letter to an old friend who had lost his brother, a Missionary in Africa, shows his old simple use of words to convey his warm-hearted love.

> I have just seen that your dear brother is gone to his rest. Dear, lovely, brave, saintly fellow! Thank God, I have prayed for him every day for years. I shall miss him in that way, but I can re-member him still. . . . Never, never was there a more unworldly, simpler, braver soul. He walked simply with God: beautiful,

lovely, steady, quiet. I do thank God that I was permitted to know him. He has always been a bright star to me.

His last Ordination came on 19 December, 1909, but he spoke to his candidates there with a hopefulness that was almost youthful: 'If you realize the promise of Christ to be with you, you not only will not be afraid, but you will cease to be surprised at the wonderful things that He will do through you.'

'I will trust and not be afraid', he wrote in his diary at the beginning of the year of his death, 1910. He knew that the end was coming but he was still wondering if he should resign, or if God would take him. With his old humility he wrote in response to the compiler of a symposium, who asked: 'What are the difficulties in your diocese?' 'Myself and my old age.' He struggled on with his confirmations through the spring, until he was really too weak to do anything but to go to his deathbed.

It was a quiet deathbed, full of loving care for many people. He said goodbye to each of his household, saying to his Housekeeper: 'My mother would be pleased to know that you are with me.'

Then his thoughts went to the Diocese; he could still dictate a letter to all his people:

My dear People,

I fear I am not able to write the letter I should wish to write. I have for some time been praying to God to tell me when I should give up my work. Now He has sent me, in His loving wisdom, a clear answer. It is a very great comfort to me to be relieved from the responsibility of leaving you. All I have to do is to ask you to forgive the many faults and immeasurable shortcomings during the twenty-five years I have been with you and to ask you to pray God to perfect my repentance and strengthen my faith to the end. All has been done in perfect love and wisdom.

My great wish has been to lead you to be Christ-like Christians. In Christ is the only hope of Purity and Peace. In Him we may be united to God and to one another.

May God guide and bless you all, and refresh you with the increasing consciousness of His presence and His love.

I am, to the end,

Your friend and Bishop.

The next morning he had his last Celebration of Holy Communion. But his love went on; one of his last visitors was a cabman who often drove him to the station, and whom he had been persuading to be confirmed. He gave him his Prayerbook. A railway porter sent him love, and had love and blessing in return. He remembered an invalid to whom he was sending an extra ration of milk; he asked that the scarlet and ermine cloak he had worn in the House of Lords should be sent to his niece, and he advised her to have it made into an evening cloak. The undertone of his thought in these last days was the perfect Love and Wisdom of God, and his trust in that was complete; and so he went forward.

'God bless you', he had written to a friend also making his last journey, 'and keep you to the end which is really the great beginning.'

'We have buried out Saint', said one of the bishops who came to his funeral.

MOTHER CECILE OF GRAHAMSTOWN

1872—1906

'THE Bishop's widows', laughed their fellow-passengers on S.S. 'Trojan' bound for the Cape as they watched the black-bonneted group of women who took their meals at the Bishop of Grahamstown's table. They formed a little group of their own on board, and the rest of the passengers fought shy of them . . . for really, those bonnets! But the more discerning of the ship's company may have taken note of a young girl among them whose grace and poise could not be disguised by her headgear. The crew, washing down the decks, noticed her sometimes coming very early to a lonely corner of the deck, where she could look out over the wide sea. If she looked up at them as they passed they were startled by the beauty of her dark eyes and her very disarming smile. What, they wondered, was she doing among the black bonnets? 'A perfect lady', they decided as they noticed her courtesy and charm. The stewards noticed that when Cecile was at a meal there was laughter and fun at the Bishop's table. What was she doing? Why was she on a boat bound for South Africa? How did she come to be among the black bonnets? She was probably considering it all very seriously herself in those early mornings when she stole up on deck to find a place to pray.

She looked back on her short life, for she was only 21, and

related it to her vocation. She saw herself as a little child, very happy, with father and mother, brothers and sisters, the youngest of the family; a bit of a tomboy, yet devoted to her dolls (she had fourteen), and specially loving flowers. She was restlessly inquisitive and determined to do just what the bigger ones did. But it ended, this dream happiness, suddenly, with her mother's death when she was eight years old; and a sad little girl used to sob herself to sleep.

She was left with a lifelong sympathy for motherless children. Home life still went on till she was thirteen, then her father died too. She had loved her parents very deeply; she often wondered what they would have thought of her present journey. Her father was a soldier, and knew about adventurous partings, her mother was an Australian belonging to that southern hemisphere to which she was now travelling. She felt that she could have been more sure of their approval than that of her brother and sister, who had made the months before sailing pretty difficult. She looked back to her school days. There was nothing remarkable about her school, but the headmistress had noticed her as a girl with a strong character. When her brother married, she went to live with her guardians in London. She would perhaps have preferred the country, as she liked things like long walks and swimming, though she never took to riding.

But London gave her the greatest thing in her life. She could never forget the cold Spring evening when she and her maid had just entered the sobriety and solidness of Eaton Square, and she noticed a light in St Peter's Church. She had persuaded the kind maid (they all liked Miss Cecile) to let her go in to the week-night Lent Service. They were rather late, and the sermon was about to begin. George Howard Wilkinson was preaching, but it was Christ the Lord who spoke in the sermon to Cecile Isherwood, sitting so quietly beside her maid; a Voice that must be obeyed and adored, a call that must be answered.

She had been used to going to St Peter's, but this service, and her preparation for Confirmation that followed it, presented her with a quite new experience of Christian Life. 'I only got hold of Christianity when I was about sixteen', she wrote later, but what a hold it was!

Her Confirmation which she remembered all her life, had been the first pledge which bound her to Christ. When she sang 'O Jesus, I have promised to serve Thee to the end', the promise, the service, and the grip of the words 'to the end' became realities to her. After that the ordinary London life seemed rather unimportant, and she accepted any little bit of service that came her way eagerly as something that she could do for the Lord.

The Brownes left London, but Cecile stayed on with a friend expecting something, she did not know what. 'Her wish', wrote that friend, 'was to give up the world and devote herself entirely to God's service.' At one time she thought of Hospital work, at another, of joining the Deaconess' order. Meanwhile she was learning from Wilkinson a deep personal religion, that love of Jesus which was to be the mainspring of her life, and she was also learning his concern for souls. When the first intimation of her real life work came to her, it rather startled her. 'I need your help', she wrote to Wilkinson. As she was praying for others who had gone overseas on a day of Intercession, she had a quite definite sense that this was to be her way. 'I have felt the call from time to time, and always shrunk back', she wrote very honestly, 'I am very much afraid of myself, yet I am anxious not to be untrue to it.'

There on the ship that was taking her overseas, she would remember that, and she could recollect the feeling that she must pledge herself so that she could not turn back, before the assault from her family set in.

It was not going to be an easy decision. 'I can never forget my agonies in 1883', she wrote later to someone who was going through the same experience. But the way of obedience suddenly became completely clear. Bishop Webb came to England from his troubled Diocese of Grahamstown, and he preached at St Peter's from the text: 'I was not disobedient to the heavenly vision'. Well, Cecile Isherwood was one who was not disobedient, though it did seem too that all her missionary longings died when she had promised to come. 'Human love, and human nature had a tremendous hold on me, and it cost not a little', she wrote to one of her sisters, and another sentence reveals what may have been on her mind on shipboard: 'Of course I feel very strongly that the very essence is the acceptance of uncertainty in all the earlier stages of vocation.'

It is worth while looking at the situation and the men that were to convince her of her vocation.

Almost everything disastrous that could happen in a diocese had happened in Grahamstown, when Bishop Webb was made its Bishop in 1882. There was such a bitter enmity between Church people that the Dean locked the Bishop out of his own Cathedral. Webb had been Bishop of Bloemfontein, and there he had established a little community of Sisters, and had learnt to depend very deeply on their prayer and dedicated lives, but at the time when he was most unhappy about Grahamstown they were unable to send anyone to help him. He came home to find the sort of women that he wanted for Grahamstown; he probably had the plan for a Sisterhood in his own mind, though he did not at once disclose it to the workers whom he had collected. Only two of them eventually made the grade, Cecile, and

Adelaide Pickthall who later joined the community. The Bishop was a man of vision. Bishop King wrote of him: 'To him the great truths of our salvation presented themselves with an ideal beauty and completeness that attracted his whole heart and mind', and King noted: 'the extraordinary spirituality and naturally soaring character of his mind.'

In Cecile he undoubtedly found someone who thought with the same rapture of holy things. He could impart things of the Spirit to her and feel that she understood, and that she had his own sense of the beauty of holiness. He had felt the quarrels at Grahamstown as a terrible disloyalty to Christ, as something for which he and others must make what reparation they might. In Cecile he recognized someone who loved Christ with the same utter devotion; as she herself was to write later: 'the Christ of St John's Gospel was the great love of my life.' Webb must have watched her keenly during that voyage, but he did not hurry her. He wanted to see perhaps if she were committed enough to stand the rather disappointing state of things in Grahamstown. For it was a very dull start, and Cecile confessed later to the little Novice Florence that she had been haunted by the feeling that 'nothing might come of this, there was so very little work at first'.

But she tackled what there was with her radiant courtesy and charm, and her passion for doing things properly, if it was only cleaning the pro-Cathedral, and taking a mother's meeting. She sped about Grahamstown with that dancing step of the saints, pouring into the troubled waters her charming manners, her humour, and her power of seeing the funny side of things. She had taken for her motto, 'Have faith in God.' Somebody wrote of her later: 'She was never sorry for herself.'

Webb was teaching her, what she afterwards handed on to

those whom she taught, that it was the life in Christ that was
first needed for all; living closer to Him would mean working
for Him even though it seemed to the world that they were
doing nothing.

Webb must have quite soon told her of his plans for a Community, for on St Mark's day 1884 she was clothed as a novice,
two other novices were clothed in the same year both older than
Cecile, and there were other workers attached to them, some
of whom later joined the Community.

Bishop Webb was quite clear that Cecile was to be their
Superior, and it says a good deal for her tact, and humility, and
love to her little group of fellow-workers that no one seems to
have minded that the youngest of the party was the leader. She
was only twenty-one, but she had a great gift for handling
people. It was partly her charm and the fact that they could see
that she set little store by her position except that she accepted
the sheer weight of the responsibility. Once later she wrote:
'It often helps me when I can't get away from responsibility, and
yet feel so sorely unequal to it, to know that these words hold
sure: "The government shall be upon His Shoulder".'

During that year the little party moved from the first little
cottage to a house which Bishop Webb had procured for them,
Eden Grove, a rambling little property with odd buildings
attached to the long, low South African house. Here the Community made its first home, with Cecile, Margaret and Charlotte as Novices, and two or three other women workers.

They were poor, even by Franciscan standards, for some
promised money was withdrawn, and the house had a mortgage
on it which had to be paid. Possibly an older Superior would
have protested against such fearfully meagre rations, and no
comforts, but they rather enjoyed the tightrope walk across

precarious circumstances. 'No words can describe the brightness of our daily life', wrote one of them afterwards. Cecile's high spirits made even the fact that they had only one rainproof cloak, and one pair of good boots among them seem palatable. One lamp lit them all to bed, and if anyone came to a meal one of the sisters had to go hungry. One wonders if the Bishop knew, but perhaps he did. As a boy at Rugby he had gone without his own meals in order to have more time for his prayers. But there were days when there was nothing in the larder and once Cecile went one way, and Margaret another to beg a little milk for Charlotte who was ill. One night when there was no money in the house, a native priest came to the door and pressed five shillings on the reluctant Cecile. 'But we are doing nothing for your people', she said. 'No, but you will', he replied. And for years the Sisters loved to remember this gift and its prophecy.

But there was one thing of which there was no shortage in the house and that was prayer. 'We must use our knees', Cecile used to say when things were desperate. One of them must go into the little chapel to pray while others conducted a difficult interview.

And from the first there were always children at Eden Grove. Cecile collected them from the prison, up to then the only place for the destitute or orphan children in Grahamstown. She had to do quite a lot of lobbying of the Assembly to get leave to do this, but she got her way.

Novice Margaret was a trained teacher, and this may have set the pattern that the Community was to follow. Cecile, one of the great pioneer women in African Education had no experience as a teacher, but a never-failing compassion for lonely and unwanted children; and the Good Shepherd School came into being. It began with one child who wrote later: 'The furniture consisted of a box on which Sister Cecile sat, having me on her knee.'

Most of the furniture consisted of boxes, and Sister Charlotte who was Irish, and whose cap was never straight, was delighted to find that her only seat was a box. (One of their voluntary workers had withdrawn her loan of furniture and they were all sitting on boxes as a consequence.) Cecile loved it because she felt that it brought closer to them the first wintry Christmas night, the manger bed, and no room in the inn. (The Community were living on her fortune, and paying the mortgage with it.)

In 1886, however, they were able to build their first chapel. It was given by Sister Margaret as a memorial of her mother; perhaps there may have been a little legacy. It became the heart of their work.

In 1886 the religious feuds in Grahamstown came to an end, and the Cathedral was once more available for its Bishop, and the Good Shepherd School, attended both by the orphans from Eden Grove and other poor children in the town, was moved into the old pro-cathedral.

Cecile had eagerly responded to an appeal to send workers to Port Elizabeth. The work there became work for the coloured children; the Community also staffed a children's ward in the hospital.

There were now eight all told in the Community, the five Novices, and three other workers. 1887 was a hard and testing year. There was illness at Eden Grove, and Novice Joan, a nurse who had joined the Community, died after heroic nursing, of an outbreak of scarlet fever. It was the year of Cecile's own profession which happened on her birthday in November, but grief and overwork had strained even her courage, and she fainted in the Cathedral. The doctor's verdict was that she must go home for a visit. The whole scheme tottered and might have collapsed, but a delicate young girl, Florence Norton, had just come out from England (against the advice of her doctors) to try her vocation. It was she who lived to be ninety and was the second Mother Superior. She arrived in time to bear Sister Margaret company during Cecile's absence in England, and to tell us in her letters home a good deal about Cecile and the tiny Community.

She was captivated by Cecile: 'The most charming, lovely, dear, sweet person I have ever met . . .' And she found the whole spirit of the home most reassuring. 'You cannot think how good everyone is to me. They take me as belonging to them and I don't seem to be at all afraid of making mistakes or doing things wrongly, as one always does in a fresh place.' Even the Bishop proved less alarming than she feared. 'He is awfully quiet and shy; it was rather dreadful at first, but when he got to speaking of real things it was lovely.'

Cecile seems to have confided to this young novice that her people in England had written to her all the first year to implore her to come back. . . . Why should she bury herself in Africa? And sadder still, 'Sister Cecile's brother and sister do not care to have anything to do with her now she is a Sister.'

It seemed dreadful news to Florence that both Cecile and the Bishop must go to England: 'What we shall do without her and him too, I do not know.' Would the line hold? Cecile must have wondered as she took ship home to England, and indeed it was something of a miracle that Sister Margaret, and the little novice, and the voluntary workers did manage to weather the next six months. They were deplorably understaffed, money was short, food was short, sickness broke out among the twenty-six orphans, and Florence went down with German measles. It is good to find that at this point the Lord sent a stout angel in the person of an old maid of Mrs Webb's, who, shod in an old pair of the Bishop's slippers, stirred about and succeeded in introducing a little solid comfort into the Home.

Meanwhile at home, Cecile was not getting the complete rest ordered by the doctor. This was one of the things that she never succeeded in doing. 'The Bishop', she wrote, 'had planned a great campaign for her', into which she threw herself and recognized with delight that her story of the start of the Community was getting home in Church circles; women were coming forward who might come back with her to South Africa, more money was available. One of the volunteers, who came out with her later, described her first interview: 'It was easy to tell her all my heart's desire; and I remember so well the look on her face as she gazed out of the window. . . . She was so fresh, so simple and natural, and seemed so unconscious of the love and joy which flowed out and made everything glad around her. Her love of truth and thoroughness impressed me, and her desire to make quite plain from the first that the life of a Sister must always be the way of the Cross, self-surrender and self-sacrifice.'

On this visit she came for the first time in contact with other Sisters. She paid a visit to Clewer, and it must have been very surprising to the mature Community there to meet a Mother Superior of twenty-five, who had directed her own Novitiate. But if they opened their eyes wide at her disclosures, they did recognize her quality, and asked her to come to their Retreat, which she found deeply inspiring; the subject was the journey to Emmaus, and she used to quote from it all her life long. She made such friends with the Clewer Sisters that she afterwards sent Sister Florence there to learn to be Novice Mistress, but she was not prepared to force her Community into the Clewer mould. She felt that they had been called to work out their own salvation, and wrote later to this Sister when at Clewer: 'We want to copy the truth, simplicity, and reality and faithfulness of the Rule at Clewer, but we must not forget that it could never be produced here. Sisters are for the Church, not the Church for Sisters, and the Church here is not ready for that; so day by day we have to learn what He would form and mould us into.' Still it must have been a strength to her to talk over her Community with other professed Sisters, and to share their life for a few days.

Such was the attraction of her own absolutely given personality that she collected eleven new workers ready to sail with her. She was full of a confidence which she tried to pass on to the much-tried stage army in Grahamstown. 'I do think if you can hold on', she wrote to them, 'that there is a bright and happy future before out little Community . . . but I can well realize what my dear family is going through now.'

She sailed at the end of 1888, bringing the new aspirants. She must have wondered if the surprising reinforcements would all materialize, for one of them wrote: 'I can remember well her expression of relief when we all turned up.' She set herself to make them happy on the voyage out, perhaps remembering some of her own misgivings. She took them ashore at Madeira for a break, and made them feel so very much her own that when poor little Novice Florence went down to the train to meet them, she found Mother Cecile so surrounded by the new entry that she could hardly get a word with her. But, oh, it was lovely to have her back, to see her standing by her own door after saying good night with an understanding word to everyone; and even if one of the newcomers had to be dismissed for dishonesty, almost at once, still most of them stayed and built up the new stage of the little Community, for 1889 was another year of surprising growth, and the great work for which the Community was being shaped began to be apparent.

The first eight years of the Community's life were over. This was the flowering . . . precarious, loving, often desperately frail and insecure. The next years, the fruit-bearing years, show us Cecile at the height of her powers, using to the full, under God, what Scott Holland called 'her incomparable charm, and her singular intellectual capacity' to perfect a twofold work.

First came the forging of the Community itself into an instrument for God. How surely this was done became apparent after her death, when the work of the Community went on without a break, and expanded in ways that she would have loved. Second to this came the discovery and organizing of the mission of the Community to South Africa, the educational work based on deep Christian teaching and example which was to become available under her leadership, for English, Dutch and Bantu. This meant a ceaseless struggle to procure buildings, to raise the money to build them, to work in with the State authorities on Education, and with other Christian bodies.

She had a passion for work to be as well done as it could be, a tremendous capacity for hard work, and a shaping mind which seized opportunities in a daring and indomitable manner. A third strain in her work was her concern with orphaned and destitute children, and the Mother Superior who had cried herself to sleep in her own orphaned childhood, continued her work for her orphan babies.

Since we are counting her among our Saints, we want to see something of her own spiritual sources.

She was outstandingly a Bible and Prayerbook Christian; and

we do not find in her life much influence of the saints and mystics. She did read *The Christian Year* to her Sisters, and sometimes quotes Christina Rossetti, but even the great *Imitation of Christ* seems to have passed her by. But over and over again, she commends to her Community passages that she has loved in the Bible and the Prayerbook collects. Above all, the Gospel of St John was her guide book, and in moments of special difficulty in a Sister's life she would suggest an intensive study of the Last Discourses, and felt that the words of Christ there would break down any resistance of the human spirit to the Will of God. Very simply she taught her Sisters to be with Jesus. He was, as she had said, 'The love of her life'. With Him she expected to endure the Cross and Passion and the triumph of the Resurrection. That was for her the essence of a Sister's life.

> We must come (she wrote to one of them) asking for the Cross, and knowing to some extent what it means. We are not Sisters of the Resurrection to escape trials, but to enable us to go forward to triumph over them victoriously.
>
> I have been thinking a great deal in my own quiet what a privilege it is for us as a Community to be allowed in any way to share the calling of the Blessed Virgin Mary to stand by the Cross of Christ. There is such a wonderful meaning for all of us in the words: 'To stand, having done all to stand.' If you and I were to know ourselves that is just the thing we find most hard—to stand by the Cross. First, I suppose because it implies that Rocklike character which can only come when we find by actual experience that we have no power of ourselves to help ourselves. We only are, or can ever really become, strong in Christ when we have learnt something of our own weakness.

She had had to take a position of authority so young, but she did it by watching Christ on His Cross, and she wrote about it once to a friend:

It is so beautiful to think of Christ on the Cross as the model for all rulers, the anxious pain, and the stretching out of the arms in entreaty and compassion, the love which won't take account of dullness or stupidity, or perverseness, which has anticipated disobedience, and gainsaying, which is not baulked by a failure or two, which goes on as if it had not failed at all, which gets no interest from its outlay of pain and grief and care, and yet hides the disappointment, and buries the bitterness. Don't you think that it is wonderful, that from the first He was tied and bound, and as we should say, so limited in His work for others?

Of her obedience, one wrote: 'I have alluded to her extraordinary devotion to our Lord. "I will guide thee with Mine Eye", this was the kind of devotion she sought and obtained. Bit and bridle were not necessary with her.' Bishop Wilkinson who knew her so well said: 'Through all ran the self-abnegation; the absolute surrender of self, the absence of self-seeking, and above all the power to work.'

And about this work one of the older Sisters testified how from the first days: 'All work started from the Holy Eucharist. Sister Cecile had her wisdom straight from the Master's hand. All things were done with prayer.'

She was a friend to so many different sorts of people. A young man wrote after her death: 'Her greatest attraction was that nothing was too bad for her. She entered into every bit of one's life, and one could tell her anything, sorrows, joys, faults, and she sympathized with everything and always saw the amusing side of everything too with that dear twinkle in her eyes. There never was, and never will be anyone quite like her again.'

Mr Bodington, who was chaplain to the Community for a few years, gives us a really understanding study of the Mother and shows a good deal of insight into her life. First he describes his first impressions of the Home.

On our way up in 1890 to our far-off country parish we stayed a few days with the Bishop of Grahamstown. I well remember one morning his proposing that we should pay a visit to St Peter's Home. We were shown into a charming little whitewashed room, and had not long to wait before the Mother Superior herself came to greet us. We were astonished. I think we had expected a venerable lady, and instead of that we saw before us a tall, supple, youthful figure, with a Madonna-like face under a Madonna-like veil. . . . Her eyes which looked through and through you were never to be forgotten, for you saw in them the Infinite through the finite. Her manners were perfect, they were the finished manners of a woman of the world, with just perhaps a touch of the purposed kindness of the saint. As she took us round her premises, she radiated an atmosphere not only of love and happiness but of life and distinction over the dullest details of the work. It was impossible to be dull where she was.

She went out once or twice to Burgersdorp to stay with the Bodingtons and, as he studies his guest, Mr Bodington wrote:

I think she was like her hero Bishop Wilkinson in that she lived her life at too great a strain. I do not mean the strain of practical energy or of intellectual activity, which did not, I think, exhaust her, but the strain of continually stretching in with her spirit after the Infinite, whether Godwards in prayer or thought or longing, conscious or unconscious, or in love towards human kind. She liked people to want what she herself could give. Life was measured out to her by the opportunity it gave of pouring herself out; in other words, life was love. The South African landscape awed her. . . . I don't think she liked the vastness of it. It seemed to add to the spiritual strain. It was too like what was going on within . . . the perpetual struggle with the Infinite. One longed to relieve her inward sufferings but it was impossible.

This intense suffering of hers had not escaped the watchful loving attention of Sister Florence who wrote home about this time: 'I do think that suffering must be necessary, because of our foundation, "Reparation to the honour of Jesus Christ". I know this thought helps Sister, only I do wish that I could take a bigger share, and she not so much, and yet we ought not to grudge suffering for our Lord to those who love Him.'

Mr Bodington wrote of her feeling so intensely the difficulties of working in a new country, difficulties in dealing with hearts that had never been grounded in an evangelical doctrine, and were so cold and hard. She had remarked that what these people wanted was the hardest the most self-sacrificing Christianity. Like most workers in South Africa, she was aware of a surrounding power of evil. 'I can only see evil at my side', she wrote, 'but however awful it may be, I do begin to believe that He will never suffer them to be lost whom He has saved.'

And to one of her Sisters she said: 'For the greatest number of His children suffering is the raw material of Glory.'

It became clear in the early 'nineties that the Community needed some sort of a constitution. It had grown up in its flowering days by a kind of divine chance, but now that it was growing bigger and its work expanding so fast, some solid foundations must be laid.

This always is a danger moment in the life of any religious venture, how to drive in the stakes, and tie back the wild growths, how to limit without destroying spontaneity. Cecile was fortunate in the three men, who with her, made a shape for her Sisterhood. First there was Bishop Webb himself. He was no organizer, but the Community was his child, and he had fostered all its upbringing. Then there was Mr Bodington, just at this time appointed chaplain for a year or two, and last there came from England in these years, George Howard Wilkinson, now Bishop of St Andrews. How important it was for Cecile to have him just at this time, how vital to the Community that these three men could work out with her a constitution for the Community which secured their freedom. But of course, they had a rare instrument in the Mother Superior. Mr Bodington remembered 'during these changes of constitution, changes most necessary, and in the end most salutary; she was at all events single-hearted in her determination to do the thing that should be most pleasing to Christ.' 'She was incapable', he wrote later, 'of taking an unintelligent view of persons or things, or one that was unsympathetic or unjust or unappreciative.'

This outlook stood her in good stead when it came to working with other Christian bodies, as her Training School work developed. She could not take up an attitude of antagonism to other Christian workers, it seemed to her contrary to the Spirit of Christ as she knew it in her heart. Mr Bodington says:

> I never remember any trouble between her and Nonconformists, indeed nothing would have pained her more. 'I am sure when we grasp what we are, we are more ready to look up to others. I don't mean Superiors, I mean the souls placed under us to train for Him. We seek the image of our Master more longingly in them, and we reverence and look up and think when we find it, however faulty the rest may be', she wrote once.

It is right at this point to consider her relations as Mother Superior with her family in the Home. As the Community grew she could not quite keep that early companionship she had had with her first Novices and Sisters, and yet her relations with them kept a delightful freshness and spontaneity, and above all a deeply affectionate, almost caressing concern for their welfare. 'My own child', 'My dearest', she began her letters, and they were full of 'Darlings'. 'You are my dearest', she wrote to one, 'I can't say more because you are each very precious to me as belonging to Christ.'

She wrote to one of them who was taking a position of responsibility:

I do believe intensely in loving truly, expecting the best, praising where one can. Then when there is need for reproof, there is to the person reproved the knowledge that personal pain has been given, not only to our love, but to our ideals for them. I would always try to love and expect again just as if the wrong had not been done. And give some little bit of encouragement to show one cares more. I fancy it is the way that God does that to us which breaks forever the hard side of the inner spirit.

But she never let them off what Jeremy Taylor called 'the honour and severity of the Christian life.'

At the beginning, she was anxious that women should not come out expecting an exotic and dramatic form of religion. She wrote soberly, 'There is no religious excitement about the Home or any part of the work, but an immense field for quiet, steady women's work.'

That is not a very typical statement but it does show her horror of the pseudo-religious.

The following is more like her own creed:

The best preparation for you for the religious life would be fully to realize that you can bring nothing but a soul and body willing to be moulded entirely anew by the Holy Spirit.

As life goes on everyday one feels more that this is the essence of a Sister's life . . . following. We begin with all sorts of self-chosen plans and ideals; gradually, as God in his infinite love and tenderness lays His pierced hand upon us, His touch claims us, then having called us, clothes us; He begins to say some of the many things He has to say to us as we can bear them, till one by one, the idols are all gone; and through painful experience we learn that we came 'not to do our own will, but the will of Him Who not only sent us, but created, redeemed, and is waiting to sanctify us.'

'Please God, and be dear to Him', she used to say to her Sisters.

The Sisters who came to find her in her own little room were sure of her welcoming attention. 'What it was', wrote one, 'to go into her tiny room, and stand a moment as she bent busily over the desk that saw such ceaseless toil, so faithfully carried out; and then to catch the sunshine of heaven as she lifted up her face. It was impossible to be with her, and yet fail to know that she had been with Jesus.'

And those who came rather nervously to try their Vocations, found the same encouraging welcome: 'We arrived, a little lonely, a little sad. How was it going to be? The Mother came along, meeting us at the station or in the hall, or in her own room . . . and the feeling was given that there was someone who was glad that we had come. She soon let us know that, yet with no gush, no effusion, but a welcome so warm, so embracing, that it awaked a response in one's own heart.'

And she filled the house with that lovely gaiety of the Saints.

She was so merry. I remember Mother coming in when five of us new arrivals were sitting about rather disconsolate; she was brimming over with laughter, and told us the joke. There was always a lot of laughter about the Mother's 'swans' who turned out to be the worst girls in the home.

We greatly looked forward to meals with Mother. She would come in and say grace very quietly, and then begin to talk in the most natural happy way, meanwhile carving rapidly and well, and remembering what each person liked. Many of us were young and would break into peals of laughter over the conversation, but Mother kept such a gracious dignity, that we never went too far. She understood youth and high spirits, and knew what to see and what not to see.

When she had to send Sisters away from her to distant work she nearly always managed to visit them. 'What happy homely little times we had together', one Sister wrote, 'how she found time to write to us as often as she did was a marvel.'

They were not easy journeys in those days.

We started as you know at 6 a.m. and arrived here at 8 p.m.! I shall never forget the heat; my cross was so hot that I could not hold it, and sun and wind both seemed like a furnace. However I feel I shall be glad all my life to have had this journey. I never before realized what the awful blaze of the Eastern sun full in the face of the Crucified must have meant. . . . There are 80,000 natives in this district alone. . . . Oh, dear child, ask God unceasingly to raise up Sisters! I am much relieved that they are building a bridge over the Keiskama river at last and none too soon. Twenty people were drowned crossing the rivers between this and Grahamstown last year, four men in the Fish river in which I came to grief. . . . I don't know what I should have done if you Sisters had had to go to and fro often, but now with three bridges there will be no risk.

Trust and simplicity, and casting of their care upon Christ, those were the things she spoke of in nearly every letter to them, and the blessed rare grace of humility.

And now we must just look at the amazing collection of fruit that followed the early flowering of the Community.

Undoubtedly Cecile was an organizer of genius. Michael Furse said of her: 'I think she was the ablest, or one of the ablest women I ever knew'. Those who knew her best used to say that she did not originate great works, but that she was capable of turning other men's dreams and visions into a reality so lovely, and at the same time practical. Give her an idea, and she would brood over it, and commit it so utterly to the Holy Spirit, that it emerged later as an actual state of things, built up into formidable strength as a weapon for God. She believed in the best that her Sisters could produce, and her faith in them did result in surprisingly good firm work. She had no use for shoddy work and her standards were high.

The extraordinary thing is, that like so many of her Victorian companions she had had almost no training in education, and yet we find her seeing how it could be accomplished and setting her hand to it with a strange confidence that if it was God's will, it could be done.

And so from the early work for the destitute children, and the little Good Shepherd School, sprang the Mission in the poorest part of Port Elizabeth, the Boarding School for the railway children and then, in 1894, the important establishment of the Training School for Teachers, the influence of which spread all over South Africa. In 1894 she also began her longed-for work for the natives. First at Herschel on the Basutoland border, then, when that proved too remote, at Keiskama Hoek. Later it was concentrated in Grahamstown itself. The Boarding School and the Training School for Native Teachers were among her darling projects, and she came to England for a short visit to collect the money needed to support them. On her return, St Peter's School became the Training College with its own fine buildings. Then began the co-operation with Dr Muir, the Minister of Education, who after having considered establishing a State Training College at Grahamstown eventually threw himself entirely into the Mother's schemes so that the training of teachers was left in the Sister's hands, and is so to this day. 'Have you', he wrote to her, 'made clear the fact that there is nothing of a speculative venture in the undertaking, that it is an assured success, that in fact it is a success which is embarrassing you, and that without increased accommodation students must be refused?'

The confidence that she had established that the Community

would offer really sound and valuable work to South Africa, was such that after her death, Sisters were sent as far north as Rusape and Penhalonga in Rhodesia, and established schools in Salisbury, and Bulawayo and many other places.

In the years between 1894 and 1898 she was able to begin the work for the natives which had always been a longing in the back of her mind and spirit. She felt violently the wrong attitude of so many people in the colony. 'The attitude about natives and native work makes my blood boil', she wrote, 'we certainly in the Church can never do enough to make up for the great wrong our white race has brought to them.'

First in the Herschel district, and then at Keisma Hoek, she planned schools for the Bantu girls: schools where they could learn to be teachers in the native schools springing up, and where they could learn the practical skills, the cooking, laundry work, and sewing which were new to them.

There was a very happy relationship between the Sisters and their pupils in these schools. Cecile herself could not often be with them but she cared tremendously about this part of the Community work, and paid them quite perilous visits from time to time over the bad South African roads.

Later, the native work was concentrated in Grahamstown when the Native Industrial School was opened there in 1902.

When the burden of building was heaviest on the Community, (writes a Sister) . . . a native girl appeared one day with her bundle. She hailed from Herschel and her name was Rebecca; she was seeking safety with the Sisters from a marriage which her family were forcing upon her. Other girls joined her and soon the authorities sanctioned this bit of native industrial work. In the thorough way that was typical of Cecile's plans she designed a three-years' course for these girls, with a certificate granted at the end.

There was so much building and new work that Mother Cecile's eyes used to twinkle as she read to the Sisters out of the Christian Year:

> Is this a time to plant and build
> Add house to house and field to field?

This is how it appeared to the vivid mind of Scott Holland in 1903.

Here we have Mother Cecile. Here *is* a personality.... It is not only the personality behind it, but here is actually a thing succeeding— a thing that is growing stronger always. Everything is growing, as hard as it can, with everybody there, and you felt the heart of it all was the beautiful Chapel with its reserve, and solemnity and its dignity, keeping the heart of the thing strong and pure and free. There is the worship, there is the prayer, and there is the beating pulse of the great faith. . . . Here is an institution of the Church which is governed by a policy which really has a mind. . . . The whole of this great work is hanging on Mother Cecile just now until it be created and made as it were. It will never really be created and established, and laid out on strong lines except by the inspiration she gives it.

This was written just after the Boer War, but we have to remember that the Sisters and their Mother had to face all the bitterness and hardship of 1899 to 1901. Mother Cecile had been home just before the War, when it seemed as if it might be right to have a Mother House in Scotland where Sisters might try their vocation before actually joining the Community in South Africa. The plan was afterwards abandoned, and fortunately Mother had got back to Africa in the early days of the War. Grahamstown was actually surrounded by the Boers in 1901, and they expected an attack which did not however happen, but they seem to have been hospitable to soldiers. Cape Town had asked her for forty beds for the wounded and St

Peter's Home had responded most heartily, Sister Anne actually nursing as well as teaching. Mother Cecile records: 'The soldiers did seem so utterly grateful and pleased for food and care. One man said, "Why, Sister, it's like a bit of real good home".' She was pleased that her pupils remained steady . . . not a lesson missed, in spite of the fact that many had had brothers and fathers fighting, and many of the farms round Grahamstown had been looted.

I suppose her greatest triumph in the War years was the regularity with which the training work went on. In 1900, in the middle of the War, they were presenting fifty-six teachers for the State examination, and fifty-three passed. The Staff was increased by Sisters who came out from the Home base. Building was being planned as usual. But Cecile was very much aware of the effects of the War. 'A. M., who lives on a farm, has just been telling us how sad the general mistrust is. It is so literally and truly a civil war in the Colony.'

She wrote letters to the Sisters whom she had left in Scotland which show how she was facing and accepting the griefs and anxieties of the War years, always with her own steadfast sense of God.

> As our nation is merged in the horrors of War one's mind goes out to the great King of Nations, remaining a King forever, sitting above the water-floods, and possibly as in the days of His earthly Ministry, pleased to find souls, faulty in themselves telling Him their needs, quietly and restfully. This power of rest in prayer will come as we let the peace of God sink into our hearts. We are some of us in such darkness, and nothing stands sure but God Himself. It is wonderful how in these sad anxious days the joy set before us does lighten the load here, and how one gets used to thinking that anything may happen to make the unseen so real, the seen so passing and trivial.

Oh, do let us in this hour of need be found faithful, really praying, and trying to do so with more surrendered hearts and lives.
It comes to me more and more each week that the special message
for us Sisters in this drawn-out sorrow is recollection . . . just the
simple increasing sense of God's own dear presence, God's own
strong supporting grace.

The anxiety is so wearing of trying to seem as if all were right
and secure; however, I only write to add that man's extremity is
God's opportunity. The difficulty does press with me a good deal.
One has to show a confidence one does not quite feel, for the
people get so terrified here sometimes.

She suffered with her girls in the Training College and had to
let them go to anxious homes. 'Many of the girls left for their
homes on Saturday morning, and the parents have the responsibility, but it does rend one's heart that some parents and brothers
are still missing.'

But she had given them some of her own 'recollection':
'The girls do seem so much in earnest, two more have just these
last days parted from their fathers who have gone to the front.
. . . In and through all I can't help a great Hope that God is going
to be exalted in righteousness.'

At the end of 1901 she was presenting more students for
matriculation in the State Examination than ever before. The
authorities were all loud in praise of the Home, and the problem
was again one of building, space, accommodation for trainees
and teachers, and the native girls coming in to their Industrial
School; and she was ill and couldn't rest in Africa. It was obvious
now that the illness which gave her so much pain was taking
hold of her, and the doctors said that she must go home, and
hoped that she would rest and have treatment. But she burnt
with such fire that she could never rest for long, especially if she
could talk to new people in England about what was happening

in Africa. Five thousand pounds was the target and how hard she worked to get it. She was told by the Bishop of Grahamstown to stay in England till it was collected, but she did so long to be back at the place that she had made into a home for so many people. 'I could literally have cried when I had the Bishop's letter asking me not to sail . . .' and again, 'How truly I can say that I would give all I know to be safely home with you instead of trying to raise money.'

But instead she remembered that it was just nineteen years since she had first sailed for Africa, and she went back to her old message: 'Have faith in God.'

She had some encouragements, a very good meeting in Oxford, at Lady Margaret, packed with students who must have felt the exhilarating charm of this saint not so much older than themselves who was claiming South African Education for God. And then the Archbishop of Canterbury (Frederick Temple) sent for her to Lambeth to hear all that she was doing, and won her heart by praying 'so beautifully' for the Community and all the children and trainees, and promised her his support.

She got back to South Africa in June 1903, and the whole personnel of St Peter's gave her a most touching welcome. Of course there was the Illuminated Address so dear to our grandparents, and all the Home was decorated. She arrived at night-time, and for a wonder in fair weather. 'The gorgeous sunset succeeded by the splendour of the moon and the starlit sky was South Africa's own reception', wrote one of the Sisters. 'Before one realized whence or how she had come, the Mother was standing on the steps of the front door listening to Home Sweet Home.'

I think physical life must have been a weariness to her from that time on. She had so much to do, so many calls for her work, and an overmastering anxiety that if St Peter's College (as it was now called) did not keep its pace, the State would set up its own schools in Grahamstown.

In the last years of her life in Africa, she was concerned with concentrating the work securely in Grahamstown. Some of the more distant ventures were given up, but substitutes were always devised nearer the Mother House. For it was finally decided that the Mother House should be in Grahamstown, and not in Scotland. It was as if she had a sense that there must be no loose ends, no place where disintegration might set in, that she must leave a manageable scheme of work for her successor.

New buildings were going up, but they were part of the solid core of the work. Only the old first venture at Port Elizabeth, with Sister Charlotte still in charge, remained at the moment outside Grahamstown.

One spiritual building on which her heart was set all the more after the War was the integration of Dutch and English girls in her Training College. She was encouraging some of her Sisters to learn Africaans. Scott Holland wrote of this:

> She had heavy on her soul the racial burden of South Africa. She recognized as inevitable the immense predominance of the Dutch in the Colony and took in the full value of their deep and tenacious virtues. She felt that the Church must not lend itself to emphasising the racial split. So she received any number of Dutch girls who would come into her family, allowing them free access to their religious pastors for instruction, and giving their pastors a very free entry into her college.

All the time her illness was creeping up on her. Sister Florence, who slept in the cell next hers, realized how many sleepless nights she was having, but spoke of the heavenly peace of her expression when she went in early to see her. They were nights spent with her Lord. But at last the pain was more than she could bear, and she went down to Cape Town for further advice in 1905.

She left the house on the last day of the Summer term, and managed an individual goodbye to all Sisters and workers who were there. They had a strange feeling that perhaps it was a last goodbye. 'We went our ways with heavy hearts, the same thought in many minds that this journey of the Mother's would be "the going up to Jerusalem".'

At Cape Town, it was obvious to her doctors that she must go home, perhaps for a serious operation. She sent for Sister Florence, her Assistant Superior, and talked over with her many future plans. 'But Mother, you talk as if you were not coming back', said the troubled Florence after one of these talks.

'It will be all right', Cecile assured her. 'God has promised me that He will look after the Community.'

(And Mother Florence in moments of stress used to find herself praying: 'O God, You Promised . . .')

When she got to England she seemed to improve in health; the doctors talked of treatment and not an operation. She went to stay with her old friends the Brownes in the house in Rolland Gardens, which reminded her of the old days at St Peter's, Eaton Square, and it was cheering to find so many friends of her work in England; but she did long for the dear family and the Home in Africa. 'Spoiling is very nice, and I do value the love and care that it all means, but the dear Home life is more than all; and every English visit makes me more thankful that one has been called to a comparatively out-of-the-way corner. There is after all more time for learning the Walk to Emmaus in our environment.'

In November her doctor's verdict was that if she would rest and avoid all fatigue she might get back to Africa in March. If she could have laid aside all effort she might have done so, but she decided in November to throw herself into one more money-raising effort for her College and its Chapel; she was visualizing an appeal for £9,000. She was even speaking for it at the Annual Meeting of her English Help Society. Her appearance shocked some of her friends who were there. Such obvious and almost painful physical weakness which for the moment robbed her of that wonderful air of confidence habitual to her . . . and then when the moment came for her to speak, the amazing beauty of her white face and glowing eyes, and the thrilling power of her voice so weakened from its old strength, as she pleaded for the work and grew strong in the pleading. She had attempted too much in this last money raising for her cause. She had given her life for it.

There was one friend whom she felt that she must see, and she ventured on the long journey to Scotland to stay with Bishop Wilkinson for a little while. It was a loving home, but perhaps not a particularly restful one, and they were tremendously struck by her interest in public affairs, and in all their doings. The two Wilkinson boys who came home for Christmas were remarkably impressed with her life and enthusiasm and goodness. She struggled up to be at the early service in the little chapel. One hears of rest on a sofa, but hardly of the complete rest that she ought to have had. However, she was getting the thing that she came for, much quiet talk with Wilkinson. He wrote afterwards of this time: 'I never knew her so near to God . . . the temptations had been conquered, the strife was practically over, the victory won.'

She wrote a final word from Scotland to those students gathering in the College for which she was giving her last ounce of health.

We none of us know what life has in store for us, but of two things we may be quite certain, if it is going to be life in any real sense: first that there will be some cross bravely to take up, something to suffer—something to bear as well as to do. Secondly, there will be an ever-increasing rejoicing in God's work, and our small share in it, and in all that goes to make up the meaning of such words as *Rejoice in the Lord*.

When she went south again, her health failed fast. She could still write to Sister Florence about coming home, but: 'I feel happier than I have ever done that we are absolutely in His Hands about it all.'

And then, after all, the severe operation was felt to be inevitable. Mr Ellison who had once been chaplain to the Community was her priest in charge of those last days, and he took down her last messages for the Community. They are so characteristic, that they must have felt very near to her when they read them.

1st.   Peg away . . . strengthening simple personal religion, in prayers, Bible reading, Holy Communion with or without feeling, earthly friendships, intercourse.

2nd.   Community life, 'If one member suffer . . .', thoroughness, sparkle.

'I asked', Mr Ellison said, 'what that last word implied, and she said at once with her old bright smile: "Oh, not to let the fun go out of the place".' She told Mr Ellison she had slept like a child those nights before her operation. 'Constantly conscious of God's presence, all through the night, and everything had been so real.' She did not survive the operation for more than a few days, but they were calm days without much pain. And then there was a collapse, and she was gone.

Her funeral service was at St Peter's, Eaton Square, and so the circle comes round to the eager girl sitting by her maid and listening to a Voice that called to her heart. At the end of the service they had her confirmation hymn, 'O Jesus, I have promised to serve Thee to the end'. Well, she had served Him to the end, glorious, wise, humble, and deeply loving service.

She wrote to the Bishop of London (Winnington Ingram): 'When one comes to stand by the river, it is a great solid joy to think of the work one has been permitted to do.' The joy of the Lord might be just that.

M

MARY BROWN

1847—1935

A WEAVER in her clogs and shawl is walking home from work in the Lancashire town of Burnley with the leader of her Sunday class. The woman with the shining eyes, the firm chin, and sensitive mouth, is the doctor's wife, and the two are evidently on the closest terms. As they part, and the girl prepares to go down the long street with the stone sets to her home, she turns to her companion and says tersely: 'Think on', and goes her way.

She knows quite well that Mary Brown will 'think on', and will remember the story that this girl has been telling her of how she is beset by attentions from her foreman, who wants to seduce her. A little later, Mary Brown begins to burn a light in her window in the tall house in Bank Parade, so that her girls, clattering by in their clogs to the mill may know that she is remembering them in her early prayers. For the clogs are her alarm clock. She always remembered the first night that she slept in Burnley, when she and her husband were awakened by a sound till then unknown to them: 'an immense rattle along the cobbled street, as though a regiment of cavalry had suddenly been let loose in the town; it grew steadily louder and louder.' Mary Brown sprang from her bed, and went to the window and there she saw the stream of men and women going to the

mills. Many of these people were later to become her friends and
disciples, for whom she 'thought on' to some purpose.

But just at first, Burnley seemed rather grim to her, so smoky
(she could see a hundred chimneys from her drawing room), so
grey, so lacking in colour.

For Mary Brown could remember sunlight, and colour, and
clear air that almost seemed a dream in Burnley. She was South
African born; her childhood's home had been in the Cape
Province, on the sea shore, with unlimited sunshine and space
and liberty. There she had grown up with sisters and brothers,
with a father, Henry Solomon, who taught her to read and
think and was always an inspiration to her, and a mother who
loved to keep open house for missionaries going and coming to
their work in Africa. Mary rembered Livingstone, and Moffat,
and what heroes they were to herself and her sisters and
brothers! It was a religious home with a father who used to pray
at Family Prayers: 'Our Father, the Father of all fathers, and of
all girls and boys.' How deeply she was to realize that later!
Then came her engagement to the young Scottish doctor, John
Brown, who was kin to the famous hero of *Rab and his Friends*.
He took the rather unusual step of sending his bride-to-be home
to Scotland; but then he was an unusual young man, and Mary's
father and mother were wise enough to see how much their
South African daughter would learn in England and Scotland.
It was the year of the Great Exhibition, and besides learning to
love Scottish scenery and sermons, and her husband's kith and
kin, Mary Solomon visited the Exhibition, heard Spurgeon
preach, and made friends with some Jewish cousins of her
father (she always valued her Jewish heritage) who took her to
the synagogue.

She came back to be married to her doctor husband in 1868,

and they went up country to a lonely practice at Frazerburg in the Karoo. This was a very different South Africa from the Cape Province of her childhood, but again a country of wide spaces and sunshine. The young doctor was popular both with the white people and the natives, who gave him all sorts of strange presents. Books were their one way of keeping in touch with modern thought, and they got a regular supply from Scotland, so that the doctor was reading John Stuart Mill to his wife in the evenings. It was in these Frazerburg years that they lost their second baby. Dr John had to dig his grave, and bury his little son without benefit of clergy, the nearest minister of religion being far away over the veldt. 'My heart is ready to break', wrote Mary, but she did not lose hold of the faith in God which her father had taught her, and she was able to comfort other troubled souls, and to share in the Quarterly Communion, the *Naachtmaal* with her Dutch neighbours. She had not yet found our Anglican Communion—that was to come later—but her father had set her feet on the road to Christ which made this time of pain and loss a growing time for her.

Her husband realized, however, that she had had a great strain, and as he wanted to keep in touch with the most advanced medicine of his day, he decided that they should go to Scotland for a time with their other children, so in 1876 they left South Africa for Edinburgh.

Two things happened to Mary Brown in Edinburgh. Her husband was busy working with Lister and Simpson, but he brought her into a circle of kinsfolk who were sincerely religious, and one of these was *the* Dr John Brown of *Rab and his Friends* whom she found wonderfully inspiring. He was an old man then, and Mary wrote of him: 'Rab is a most delightful and wonderful man, with his gentle tender face beaming with sympathy. I had never met anyone like him before, the beauty of his own soul makes him see the beautiful in all around him, and just because he is not an ordinary man one feels free to tell him things garnered and sacred to one's own heart alone.' One day he took her for a long drive in the rain in an open trap, but they were so intent on their talk that she scarcely noticed the rain. 'I never met anyone who calls forth so readily the love and tenderness of one's nature as he does', she wrote after that day.

The other experience struck at her heart. It was in Edinburgh that she began to realize the misery that immorality and drunkenness were causing in human life. Her husband had thought that she might train as a midwife so that she could help him if he went back to a lonely South African practice. The theoretical part she had mastered, but when she came to do the practical work in the hospital wards her deep sympathy discovered such misery among the unmarried mothers that she could not finish her course. 'You'll get used to this sort of thing', her husband told her; but she cried out, 'I never will. From this day I'll fight against the degradation of women and men.'

She began her fight in the slums of Edinburgh which was a fairly stiff school at that date. She went to help people where no other women would venture, and began there her enthusiastic work for temperance. When she left Edinburgh for Burnley she felt herself a dedicated person. She was longing for home life after her husband's student life, and when the chance came of sharing a practice in Burnley, they took it, perhaps at that time meaning to return to South Africa sooner than they did. As they travelled down to the Lancashire town Mary fell into talk with a working man in the train: 'Aye, Lancashire folk are a bit rough but I tell you Missis if you find t'way to their hearts, they'll keep you there.' How true that was to be for her she scarcely guessed.

They were kindly received at Burnley, at the old Parish Church where Mary was soon given a class of girls, and also by neighbours with gardens, Shuttleworths at Gawthorpe and Thursbys at Bank Hall, and Mary found green places where she could take the children. Burnley was not a huge town; it was possible to get out into hayfields in those days. But the doctor's house was right in the middle of the town. Their first years were rather hard ones as the Bank in South Africa holding all their savings failed, and Mary had to turn to in the house and do without much help. Only Dr Mackenzie who came to work with John knew of all her economies. It was a good house, and she always remembered with pleasure her upstairs drawing room which she made such a centre later for all sorts of people. There was often a book standing open on the chimneypiece, perhaps Walt Whitman whom she loved, or Edward Carpenter, and she refreshed herself with snatches of reading while she worked. 'There are times', she wrote, 'when nothing quite suits my moods but Walt Whitman or Edward Carpenter. Indeed they both have been as saviours to me, many times saving me from myself and other little things.' Sometimes Burnley and the smoke and grime oppressed her beyond belief, but then she would go and find someone more wretched than herself to comfort and to help. She had some old friends living in cellars to whom she took food and flowers, and sometimes she would hire a cab and drive them into the country.

What time she could spare from her children in the early days in Burnley she gave to the girls in her class. She took to meeting them on Saturdays as well as Sundays. One day two young men came to her. 'There are girls', they said, 'who work in our mills that we call Mrs Dr Brown's disciples. They are different, and it's all because of you. We want you to come and speak to us young men, so that we may be better company for them girls.'

So she went and spoke to seventy or eighty young men in the room belonging to the Wesleyan Chapel. She had chosen for her text the line of Tennyson: 'Live pure, speak true, right wrong, follow the Christ'. She had gone to the trouble to have these words printed on little cards which she gave to her young men. Years afterwards, she was to see one of these cards framed in a happy home.

Work for Temperance was her next big adventure. It was a live enough issue in Burnley, where drunkenness was wrecking many homes. Mary came up against it through what she afterwards called her Wicket Gate. She was walking home one day, and saw a little shop with some rather attractive sweets in the window that she thought she would buy for the children. She went in and found the shopkeeper, a woman of about her own age, in tears. People in trouble generally managed to tell their griefs to Mary, and this woman had a piteous enough story of a drunken husband now in prison, but shortly to be released. Mary promised to come and see him when he got home, and, fulfilling this promise, took a chance and asked him if he would take the pledge. 'Hast thoo iver takken it?' he asked, and she there and then offered to take it with him so that they could fight the battle together. 'Now we stand shoulder to shoulder to fight this thing out', she told him. And so they did, for as long as she could hear anything of him, he kept sober. This little incident made rather a stir. 'T'new Doctor's wife is Temperance', people said, and it led on to her standing in front of the battle for temperance, though it was rather a rare thing for Church people in Burnley to commit themselves in this way; most of the leaders were Nonconformists. She came to a moment that was no Wicket Gate, but a full-scale Hill Difficulty. There came to Burnley two women well known in those days as Temperance leaders (one was a sister of John Bright), and they asked for a platform of Burnley women, and for a chairman selected Mary Brown. Should she dare to do it? Would it hurt her husband's practice? She went for advice to her parish priest Canon Parker, and he said rather courageously: 'There may be some poor devil in the audience whom you could help, so you had better do it, and good luck.' So Mary, putting on her best coat, embarked on her first effort at public speaking. As she addressed the meeting she suddenly realized a 'call'. She wrote afterwards, 'I suddenly became conscious of power, that I had a mission among these men and women, a mission of love and sympathy.' With her call came also a sense of deep humility . . . so that was why she was in smoky Burnley, far away from her sunshiny South Africa . . . she was there to help people . . . only how did one help people? . . . only as one took a very humble position, as she remembered later when she read some words of Edward Carpenter: 'Can you be yourself one of the lost? Arise then and become a Saviour.'

The Browns did another unfashionable thing when they espoused the cause of the Co-operative Society. In the days when they were hard up, when they first came to Burnley, they found that they could deal with profit at the Co-op. It was another link for Mary with the Burnley women to stand in the queue with them in their shawls and clogs, and take her turn at the counter. To her the Co-op, and later the Women's Co-operative Guild were part of her call. It was because she had stood in the queue with them that some of the women who belonged to the Co-op came to ask her to get a Guild started for them. Part of the Co-op profits were allocated in those days to club work, libraries and lectures. Under the leadership of Margaret Llewellyn Davies, the women had begun to share in these privileges, and to have their own Guild. Mary Brown's second effort at public speaking was more stormy than her first, and it was no occasion for her Sunday coat. The women had posted themselves in the first row of the Annual Meeting, and from her seat there, Mary rose to ask that some of the dividend might be alloted to a Woman's Co-operative Guild. There was a murmur of dissent, but one voice cried, 'Get on a chair, we can't see tha.' So Mary stood on her chair and bravely pointed out that it was the wise spending of the women that made the success of the movement. She felt the power again, as she moved that hardheaded meeting to consent to their women starting their Guild. She was its president for years, and it brought her into the closest touch with Burnley women. A little pamphlet has survived that she wrote for them, to show us how she got across her longing to make women's lives as creative, lovely and responsible as she could, to carry forward that fight to which she had vowed herself in the Edinburgh Maternity Hospital.

Let us hold family life sacred, for it is of God. Human thought or Human conception did not originate family life. Long before there was either Church or State it existed, and through all time woman has been the centre of its strength, its sweetness and its power.

It is the very sacredness and earnestness of a woman's calling in the home that fits and prepares her to work beyond it, and we shall find that the more women rise to the fullest development of their nature they will better take their position in the destinies of the world.

Every woman should if possible belong to some outside Organization that will help and enable her to bring some change and freshness of spirit into her daily life. It is in having some larger interests that one keeps free of the small things that drag a woman down, and often cramp her sympathies and endeavours.

Women must remember that it is in the home that the men and boys are strengthened for the conflicts of life, and it is necessary that the wife and mother keeps her ears and eyes open as to what is going on in the world outside.

To step beyond the home life requires both faith and judgment and a willingness, if need be, to be misunderstood in carrying out what has come to us in the clear light of duty.

But her work in Burnley was not only concerned with women; her *Call* was more general, and some of her most outstanding work was with men. We have noted the young men who came to ask to be made the right mates for her disciples. Mary had a seeing eye for those who needed help, and she saw in a gang of roughish men employed by the Corporation of Burnley in laying the rails for the new tramlines, some homeless, rather reckless souls who needed her care. She felt that they were just being used as tools to complete a heavy job, and that the town owed them more than that. So with four women friends, she organized a little homely service for them on their lonely Sundays to which they were invited to come in their working clothes. Surprisingly enough, seventy to eighty of them turned up at the first meeting. They liked the warm room, and the cheerful hymn singing, and the short talk from Mary, and it was here she found two men, stalwart helpers for her future work in Burnley. Harry Gibson and Charley Bray belonged to the gang, and Mary's friendliness penetrated to them. She had had a word with Harry, suggesting that he should take the pledge, and he had consented, with rather wry doubt as to whether he could keep it. She got a further link with him when the ladies gave out small Testaments to their guests at the meetings, and Mary gave one of hers to Harry. The gang dispersed and that bit of Mary's work seemed over, but one day she met Harry Gibson with his mate Charlie in the street in Burnley and noticed that he was wearing, as she was, the Blue Ribbon of the Temperance movement. He greeted her, and began to talk as people found they could talk to Mary. He confessed that at first after he had taken that pledge it had not gone too well with him, but then he had signed on again with a body of Temperance workers. It seemed natural for both these men to tell Mary that they had been converted, that God had come into their lives, and Harry said that it was all that Testament she had given him that had begun it, and would she come now and see his wife and his home. It was a poor home she found, the two men had only one top coat between them, but from then on, they constituted themselves her bodyguard when her calls took her to roughish spots. She felt the reality of their faith and recognized them as the saints and heroes that they were. Dr Brown must have been glad that she had such a bodyguard, for her next concern was with a rough lot of navvies building a reservoir some two miles from the town. She used to go up to them every Sunday, rain or fine, and either Harry or Charlie went with her. She gave them a talk, shared their dinner, and read to them or let them sing. They looked for her coming, and she discovered afresh the power that had come to her at the Temperance meeting to reach them and talk to them. Once, in the middle of her talk, a very rough and very drunken ganger came in spoiling for a fight. Some of the men rose to turn him out, but Mary asked them to leave him alone; however, when he threatened to disturb all that she was trying for, she went down to the door herself and putting a hand on his shoulder, put him out with a dexterous little push. It was a great joke among the men, 'how Mrs Dr

Brown put ganger Bill Jones out of t'spot . . . and in her gloves too.' He came back very penitent the next Sunday, and hung about the door till Mary went out to bring him in, and told him they were all waiting for him. Well, he came in, and such was her power, that he came into Temperance too. On the last Sunday of their stay when she had driven up, the men took the horse out and pulled her back to Burnley.

It was in Burnley that she began a work that seemed to her the most searching, and demanded most from her. Ellice Hopkins, the great Moral Welfare pioneer, had been a heroine of hers ever since Edinburgh days, and now when Ellice Hopkins visited Burnley she found in Mary a disciple ready to do the spade work in starting a House of Help for girls in moral danger. It was a new sort of work then, and rather suspect among the respectable, but some of her Burnley friends, notably Lady Shuttleworth, backed up the new venture, and the house was opened. They found the work there a difficult proposition, as it always is, so hard to staff, so full of desolating surprises, as well as reassuring rewards.

Mary tackled it at its deepest levels.

It was in the Lock ward of the Burnley Infirmary (she wrote) that I saw so much of the degradation of women. It was a practical demonstration of what I had read in Josephine Butler's life and in that book of Stead's. . . . If the Temperance cause had roused me to action, this—the social evil touched me far more deeply. It appealed to the very highest in me, and somehow those wretched girls in the Lock Ward never repelled me. . . . I believe some are chosen to suffer, and I know I was chosen for this particular *Via dolorosa*.

She often felt the evil as almost a stain on her own life, and confessed that she couldn't have stood up to it if it had not been that she could come to make her Communion. 'Those early services at the old Parish Church were an inexpressible help and comfort to me. There were times when all I was seeing and hearing seemed to smudge me, and to depress and darken my spirit, and those early services were my one comfort. It was as if a cleansing hand had passed over me.'

This work for girls brought her into contact with another group of men, as she began to see the chances that the police had of helping these desolate women. So she bravely started a class for them. 'I've begun my class for the police' (she wrote to a friend). 'I never undertook any work feeling more my own insufficiency.'

Twenty police came to the first class, and the course went on for some time. It resulted in more and more work for herself, for the police brought her all their hard nuts to crack. It was because she was so human and natural as well as so full of the Spirit that she reached people. There was one family where the father had periodical bad bouts of drinking, and a cowed little girl would come up to Bank Parade to ask if Mrs Brown could come down because: 'Ee's been sooping again.' She went down one time and found him in a particularly truculent mood. He wasn't going to be said by any woman, he'd drink as much as he wanted. Mary turned away and went over to the fireplace and leaning her head on it burst into tears. 'Nay, woman, thoo shalt niver shed another tear for me!' cried the man in distress, and he gallantly kept his word.

All sorts of people came to the tall house in Bank Parade, for she gave much hospitality to speakers for causes that appealed to her; General Booth came with his son—and turned the house upside down—Margaret Llewellyn Davies, Mrs Aveling (Karl Marx's daughter), Lady Henry Somerset, Margaret Macmillan,

W. H. Stead, besides Anglican Sisters interested in rescue work. 'This is a funny house', she wrote once, 'Sister Teresa and Miss Hartley were here discussing work for girls, when my son came in and said, "Mother, there's a Salvation Army Captain wanting to know if you can billet their Colonel." So, as the Anglican Sister departed the Salvation Army Colonel came in.'

When her work with the navvies was over, she gave her Sunday afternoons, when her maids were out, and she could open the door herself, to a group of working men, who came to talk, and to borrow books, and to be read to. They were a most varied set, men who would later have got what they needed from the W.E.A., but who now had no chance of it in Burnley except in this upstairs drawing room, where they felt free to talk and discuss, and to find out a little about poetry and general literature.

How did she fit all this in with her home life? The children were at boarding school before the main spate of work descended on her. While they were little, her chief work was with the girls. Her husband was always interested in what she was doing. His own work linked with hers. The children remember their father coming in from the surgery where he had a lass waiting 'wanting the river' because he had had to tell her that she was going to have a baby. Mary was quick to make up a bed, and kept her in their house as a guest. It was before the 'House of Help' days and made her see the need for it, but it was still another use for their spare room. One thing the doctor did count on and which she always managed to provide for him, was his rubber of whist on Saturday evenings, and she kept her Saturday evenings for him. They talked over their various problems together, and remained everything to each other, in a singularly happy marriage; but he must have been an unselfish and generous man to give her so readily to so many claims. Of course as a Victorian professional man's wife she had two maids, with whom she was on the most affectionate terms, and she writes of reading aloud to them, and seeing that they had books that they liked.

It was the Co-op members who chose her to be the first woman guardian in Burnley in 1894. She had been a visitor at the Workhouse from her first days at Burnley, when Lady Shuttleworth had begged her to take on this particular job. But women guardians were a rarity in Lancashire, indeed she was one of the first, and some of the men guardians were not very happy about it. 'But my nomination paper is signed, and everything is in order', she wrote. 'My canvassers are all working men and women. I have been a little surprised to find that several of my better-class friends held back from signing my nomination paper.'

She didn't go out to canvass on the election day, but was sitting most peacefully waiting for the results, when there was a clatter of clogs on the stairs, and a voice cried out that 'Mrs Doctor Brown had come out ont' top of t'poll.'

There was plenty of work for the new guardian to tackle. In the nursery, four babies lay together in a huge wooden cradle; a consumptive girl of fourteen was sewing something. Mrs Brown enquired what the work was, and the answer came: 'Shrouds, that's what them is, and a fine hand she is at it.' Consternation was registered in the Board Room when she asked for tooth brushes for the children: 'What, is each child to have one?' the men guardians asked in horror. There were only pauper nurses in the Infirmary, and no trained head of the wards. Mrs Brown was joined by other women guardians later. At the end of her term of office, a new Infirmary had been built with trained nursing staff installed; five cottage homes had been built for the children and staffed by good foster-parents. But the whole system went against the grain with her, and she prayed and hoped that the day would come when workhouses as work-houses would pass away. 'Meanwhile' (she wrote) 'I shall be content to attend to the needs of the sick and old, the children, and the feeble-minded, and to bring a new spirit into existing conditions.'

How much she sensed the longings in people's hearts may be shown by a story she wrote down herself, of an old Scottish woman in the Workhouse who hungered for the wide moors of her girlhood and for the heather. It was like Mary to write off to a nephew in Scotland and ask for a bunch of heather from these same moors, and when she took it to the Workhouse she recorded:

Margaret was sitting as usual, bending over her sewing, and she did not notice until I was near. Then she glanced up and saw me, and yet she did not—she looked past me. A strange twitching, half smile, half pain came over her dear old face, and dropping her work she sprang forward. The wrinkled hands stretched out with a child's eagerness. 'Eh, heather, heather', she said—'heather from my own Lammermuirs!' and with a sort of sob she buried her face in the bunch and said, 'Aught mile o' heather around my father's cottage. Eh, woman, you've made me glad the day.'

Another friend in the Workhouse was old Sammy, also Scottish. 'He was so clever, so well read, so wonderful as a reciter of Burns. I remember him once reciting something from *A Cottars Saturday Night* when he became suddenly transformed. Fire and passion, tenderness and eloquence all mingled as the rich Scot's voice rose and fell.' Well, on his death in the Workhouse she felt that she must go to his funeral, and she took with her a wreath of primroses that she had made for him. When she laid it on the desolate pauper's grave she noticed a woman from another funeral group watching her. 'Did yon belong to you?' asked the woman, and when Mary told how he was an old man that she knew in the Workhouse, and that she couldn't let him be buried without someone to follow, the woman put her hand on Mary's shoulder. 'God bless you, woman, for what you have done today.' It was like that with Mary; she stirred that life of God which was in the poor, the desolate, and the sad: they recognized something beyond them.

All her going and coming with the poorest of the poor in Burnley, did not make her lose her appetite for lovely things, or appreciate less the chances of meeting distinguished people, which came to her through her friendship with the Shuttleworths of Gawthorpe. 'I would plunge', she remembered, 'from scenes in the Workhouse, or a wild expedition among navvies working on the great reservoir, or from a meeting of our Co-operative Guild to a dinner party at Gawthorpe where we heard much of the best books, of politics, of social questions and music.'

There she met Judge Hughes of *Tom Brown* fame, Sir Edward Grey and his lovely wife whom she took to see a mill and a workhouse, and Bishop Fraser who had confirmed both her and her husband.

Perhaps the most understanding thing that the Shuttleworths did for her was to release her from the grime and stress of Burnley for a while, and take her to Italy, and she burst out: 'Oh the joy and the rapture of those Italian skies after years in Lancashire and Scotland.'

She had an afternoon that she never forgot on that visit with George Macdonald, then in the height of his powers, and heard him read to his guests. She had taken her Walt Whitman with her, and the Open Road was frequently in her mind.

> Along the 'Open Road' I saw so much, such wonderful things. I saw in the eyes of the peasant woman the same light and tenderness, and wistfulness that I had seen in the eyes of our Lancashire toilers. I saw in the refinement and culture of those with whom I moved the same need of love and sympathy and understanding that makes all human beings one.

The Burnley years were broken into by a journey to South Africa in 1898. Before studying this return, it is vital to look at whatever Mary Brown revealed of the sources of her deep compassion, and her creative energy, and of her power of understanding those around her. As in all our nineteenth-century saints, her faith was a fire, lighting and directing whatever she did, and also inspiring those who knew her. Her compassion was truly a suffering with those who appealed to her for help; she was alive to the Cross wherever she found it. Her religion was inclusive; it had come from so many sources, from her father, with his Jewish Christian outlook, from the mystical Presbyterianism of 'Rab' and from the welcoming Anglicanism of St Peter's, Burnley. She was nourished by all Christian thought, by Quakerism, by Roman Catholicism and the Salvation Army. But she nevertheless held quite firmly, after her confirmation by Bishop Fraser, to what she called our own Church. She was very sure of her foundations; 'Christ is God', she held, 'for no power of evolution could have evolved so great a force, so infinite a compassion, so gracious a Presence.'

> If you really want to know what I believe, I must say that I believe that Jesus Christ is the Light that lighteth every man that cometh into the world, if that man or woman will take His life and study it, and try to live it, not study it through books but out of the simple

Gospels. The marvellous thing is that wherever Christ is truly accepted and loved, men grow purer and nobler and the Kingdom of God is made visible here on earth. To reject Christ seems to me like shutting oneself out of the Light of Life, to accept Him is to bring infinite capacities for love and gladness into life. . . . Our lives must shew our creed. Truly I believe that Jesus Christ is the only Master worth serving. Act as though He was, and you will believe that He is.

In one of her campaigns she wrote: 'Let us work towards this issue with faces lifted towards the Infinite Goodness, towards the Light that streams from Calvary.'

It was in this way that she worked, looking at the infinite goodness, believing in the light that shines from the Cross.

The journey to South Africa was taken at a troubled time; the crisis of the outbreak of the Boer War was coming nearer; the Jameson raid had already bedevilled the issue. The Browns had an introduction to Kruger, and went to see him when they arrived at Pretoria.

I was much impressed by the old man (wrote Mary) and that impression carried me beyond any prejudices or calumnies that were so liberally bestowed during the war of 1899-1902. I came away with a feeling of great respect and pity for that old man . . . one looks back and sees the forms of Paul Kruger, Rhodes, Chamberlain, all intriguers, but I think the hands of the old Boer were the cleanest.

One of the people who had deeply influenced Mary Brown was Olive Schreiner. She had met Olive at Frazerburg in the early days of her marriage. They had confided their hopes and ambitions to each other, and had kept up the friendship. Mary felt the amazing power of the delicate South African woman. It was to Mary Brown at Burnley that Olive Schreiner sent the untidy manuscript of *The Story of a South African Farm*. Mary felt that the very leaves of the book had a smell of South Africa, and she read it with a strange emotional longing for her own country. The Browns sent it through a friend, to a publisher in Edinburgh. He was struck by it, but recommended certain alterations, and the book was sent back to Olive who later brought it herself to England where it was published by Chapman and Hall. But she was struggling all the time with terrible asthma and couldn't realize her dreams of work—writing and nursing. 'Our friendship', wrote Mary, 'was founded upon mutual sympathy and understanding of each others ideals, and on mutual respect and love. If I were asked what was the greatest characteristic of her nature, greater even than her genius, I would say her capacity for loving.'

Now that she was back in South Africa and Olive was in England, Mary wrote: 'Tell Olive everything she ever said of this land of Karoo, and sky and hill is true.'

This return to her native land was a time of great growth in spirit for her; she found herself needed and able to help South African women, as she spoke to them several times about temperance and moral welfare. 'I'm longing to tell you' (she wrote to a friend) 'of the wonderful time I am having, of the love, sympathy, and tenderness which is an inspiration. It is all beautiful, and there is a calm about our meetings, an underlying sense of peace which makes me feel that I am near God all the time.'

She felt very much the pull of her own country. 'South Africa is growing dearer to me every day. My love for it tingles all through me. I have had such a time of giving and getting.'

This visit to South Africa was important for both her and her husband, and made them eventually decide to go back and make their last home there.

When the Browns came back from South Africa it was not to return to the tall house in Bank Parade, but to a small house on the Gawthorpe estate. It was near enough to Burnley for her to go on with some of her work there; but it was a place of sorrow for her. The mother who had laid her first little son to rest at Frazerburg, now had to lose another son who came home only to die. Her loss called out very much love and sympathy from her Lancashire friends, but it was grievous to her.

She was also very unhappy about the Boer War. She had such sympathy with the South African Dutch that she could never reconcile herself to the fact that England was at war with the Boers. Her heart was in the South Africa that she loved and it broke her to know that English and Dutch were fighting each other. She shared this misery with Olive Schreiner, and it deepened the bond between them. To make some break in this double distress Dr Brown took her abroad. He had finished his work as a General Practitioner, and they felt free to spend a good deal of time in Italy during the next two years. In Florence she made a good many Browning pilgrimages, for both Brownings had inspired her from girlhood onwards. So she went to the Casa Guidi Windows, to Mrs Browning's grave, to the street corner where Browning had bought the MS. that was the origin of *The Ring and the Book*. While in Florence she also made a pilgrimage to the Ghetto. Her Jewish ancestry meant much to her and the afternoon she spent in the Oltre Arno gave her a thrill, and a deep regret for the missed vocation of her race.

It was in Italy that she met Keir Hardie whose ideals touched her own at so many points. She saw him one afternoon raising his hat to an old Italian woman with her load of faggots. He was ill and badly lodged, and the Browns persuaded him to come and share a villa which had been lent to them. This friendship gave her a new insight into the aims of the Independent Labour Party. When she saw him again later in South Africa, she wrote:

> It meant so much to clasp his strong true hand again, and to see the light in his brave clear eyes. It wasn't only seeing and touching the man, it was coming into contact with all that he stands for. . . . I don't know if I think of this great spirit as Socialism. I suppose it must have a name, but I rather think of it as a new dispensation, a cleansing fire that will burn up the dross and stubble of our modern civilization, and make plain a highway for the coming of the Lord. Of course one sees the best of the movement in a pure altruistic soul like Keir Hardie's.

The Browns went back to South Africa in 1905. They had a married daughter there to welcome them, and so the circle of Mary's life was rounded off as they came back to the Cape and Rondebosch.

Probably they had thought of the move as leading quietly to retirement; Mary was nearly sixty and her husband a little older, but for her it turned out to be only a new plunge into leadership.

It was Temperance work that first claimed her; but no body of women led by Mary Brown could stop short there. The Women's Christian Temperance Union of Cape Colony were not long in appointing her as Superintendent of their Department of Social Purity and Moral Education, and her work on this post was eventually extended to all the Union.

Work for inebriate women, work for the feeble minded, the editing of the Society's paper, *the White Ribbon*—all became alive when she touched them. She was much more than a committee woman. Her home was the place to which all sorts of people came for help and advice. 'This little house', she wrote, 'is like a signpost on the highway, or like a lighthouse to wrestlers on a stormy sea. I thought I was going to be quiet for the rest of my days, but have been once more called to active service, and the need for workers is so tremendous.'

And she regretted the way the English people in the Union were content with sport, and bridge, or journeys to England— 'so much philanthropy lost in the deep sea between the Cape and Europe', she felt.

Her call to care for girls was renewed in those South African years. She talked about Moral Welfare up and down the country; to students at the Mother Cecile Memorial Hall at Grahamstown, to Army wives at Cape Town, to a body of Dutch women at Bloemfontein. She began to be a sort of legend in the Union, this frail-looking woman in her grey dresses and white fichus, who could talk on the most sordid subjects, and suddenly transfigure them with a vision of what might be.

It was costly work, for her health was not so good as it had been. One journey, from the Cape to Johannesburg to help in a Moral Welfare Campaign, was undertaken when she was in considerable pain after an accident.

After all (she wrote) my aches and pains are my own, and I can offer them up on the altar of humanity and country. I firmly believe that the days of martyrdom for principle and for Christ are not past, and in the conflict of right over wrong we who bear Christ's name will have to bear something definite for His sake: fatigue, misgivings, misrepresentations, all sorts of things. . . . I shrink from this like a little David going against a Goliath, but the battle must be fought, and I am the chosen leader. I did not choose myself. It is strange and bewildering to me to think of the position I hold in the country. It overpowers me, and I feel so humbled and yet so strengthened for every time such a call comes I think it may be the last. Necessarily, and naturally the sword must soon drop.

She shrank from nothing that South Africa presented in the way of human problems—White Slave Traffic, all the complexities of the Colour problem, the Raising of the Age of Consent, the panics about assaults on white women by the natives. She induced General Botha to include women on the commission he set up to enquire into this last question, and made him admit the value of women in the study of social questions.

One thing she and Mother Cecile held in common; both realized the deep worth of the Dutch women, and the part they could play in the coming years. She went up to speak to a gathering of them, the Africaansche Christelyke Vrouwens Vereenigen. She could not give her address in Africaans, and her speech had to be interpreted sentence by sentence. She was not well, and the effort was great. But she reached their hearts by speaking first of all of her young married days in Frazerburg, of her Dutch friends there, of the *Nachtmaal* she had shared with them, of their kindness to her in her early bereavement. So the contact was made and 'the dear solid strong woman who never moved but only listened' were inspired by the slight vital woman who spoke to them in such a spirit of friendship. She realized that she was being used as an electric force to set forward a whole new movement. 'It was a long way to go to deliver a message, but it was well worth while . . . underneath all was the sustaining love and prayer, and the work was accomplished.'

There were, of course, times of relaxation in her South African programme, especially in her daughter's home in Durban, where there were darling grandchildren for her to enchant, as she had enchanted children all her life through, telling them stories and making paper toys.

The 1914–18 War, with all its exultations and agonies coincided with a much lower level in her own health, but she emerged to speak at a meeting when Lady Buxton was forming the League of Honour at Cape Town, and she spoke also to the soldiers—looking, so someone said, like a little grey mouse in her silvery dress and white hair. But it was a most unmouselike speech. 'One knows no self and no fear when one realizes the issues at stake', she wrote. She was conscious that they wrestled not with principalities and powers, but with spiritual wickedness in high places.

In 1917 she and Lady Buxton were again speaking together in Durban to protest against certain houses of illfame, and speaking so forcibly that some of them were closed immediately. She went on from Durban to Heilbron, Bloemfontein, and Kimberley. 'Three hundred young people . . . 105 men at the meeting for men, and a crowd of women yesterday', she records. 'John and I are to stay with the Bishop of Kimberly, so I finished up in the arms of my own Church. Keep me in your prayers.'

One of the things she longed for in South Africa, was a really beautiful service: 'It is curious how I wish more than anything else for a beautiful Church service. . . . Church life is such a struggle here, such poverty, such limited means for needed great endeavours.'

After the Kimberly meetings, a Boer wrote to her about a group of men who had heard her message. 'We are prepared to fight for you at any time . . . satisfied to give up our position or our life, to balance the position of women and men: Yrs., Madam, ready to die for you . . .'

Lady Buxton, who worked with her at this time wrote: 'Her belief was like a flame. To be with her was to be taken into a different world—a world of values quite beyond those of ordinary life.'

After 1917, it became difficult for her to do active work, though she did appear once or twice to speak for things that she loved. She still felt that she could 'pass on ammunition from the back line'. Indeed her influence, and her fire of love were very present with those in the front line, and her own power of intercession seems to have grown and deepened in those years when she could not come and go as before.

She and her husband kept their golden wedding together in 1919. He wheeled her to early Communion in her chair, and love poured in on them from every side. One of the things she treasured was a letter from one of her old friends among the navvies at Burnley.

In the last few years of her life when she was crippled and nearly blind, still more people came to ask for her help, and to talk to her. C. F. Andrewes brought two Indians who had come over to the Indian Conference. 'They sat around her wheeled chair', wrote a friend who was there, 'drinking in every word the little hostess said to them.' At the end of the talk she said: "Oh, I have much to learn!" But Sastri, one of the Indians, bowing his head over her hand said, "And to teach".'

They were well served in their last years, the doctor and his wife who had served others so faithfully. Years ago in Frazerburg, Dr Brown had ushered a coloured baby into the world, who when she heard that these two had come back to South Africa, went to them and worked for them with great devotion for eighteen years. Arlie Peterson saw them through to the undefeated end.

When Mary Brown was seventy-nine and a complete invalid, she wrote:

The springs of youth come bubbling up in the most unlooked for directions. I am never lonely, and some of my best thoughts come when I am lying awake at night. . . . It often comes over me with such a strange feeling that I will never read my Bible or look up references again. It seems almost impossible, but I'm thankful I know so much by heart.

Her husband went on before her, but in the year or two that remained to her she was still thanking God for the love of those who prayed for her, for heavenly power given to her every day, for the continued gifts of thought and memory, and above all for sense of light ahead, the *Lux Perpetua* that would make her last journey bright with hope.